PRAISE FOR HEART V,

Reading *Heart Value* feels like an adventure that guides you to pull out your good traits and then places them center stage and breathes new life into them. It's a huge confidence builder, and Mary Tess guides readers as if she were their best friend, offering heartfelt advice for their highest good.

—Linda Dickinson

Wow—before this book, I didn't realize how often I led with logic or incorporated other people's influences into my decision-making process. In many ways, *Heart Value* opened my eyes and gave me courage to show up and share my value with this world based on what energizes me.

—Eugene Murphy

I may get a tattoo that says "Freedom to Choose Again," because I've often forgotten that I don't have to live with a choice that doesn't feel right long-term. I also love this idea that we're constantly accruing value and that every experience—the good, the bad and the ugly—is a worthy investment in my Value Vault. *Heart Value* offers simple and relatable concepts that apply to many areas of life. It's a must-read!!

—Katie Delnero

Mary Tess's gentle, funny, straightforward and vulnerable voice creates a safe place to explore my perceptions of, and beliefs about, value. She generously backs up her stories and conversations with reflection and discovery exercises to create even more awareness of what has made and will make a lasting impact on my life.

—Joey Masiuk

Heart Value is a robust yet accessible guide to unlocking the value we offer that lights us up. I highly recommend Mary Tess's work to anyone who feels deflated or overlooked and wants to feel appreciated in ways that matter.

—Kim Woodworth

Heart Value is an easy and relatable read that encourages us to challenge antiquated thinking and resist negativity so we can create, refine and discover our own life of resonance. Mary Tess goes beyond directive telling and presents powerful coaching questions and thoughtful activities to inspire each reader and invite them to discover what is calling.

—Jeffrey Shaw

Heart Value is the ultimate guide for readers who want to identify and understand what they value most, which leads to deeper connections and appreciation at home and work.

—Ingrid Nelson

As an avid reader of personal development books (Tony Robbins, Stephen Covey, etc.), this is now my favorite book. I thought I was doing what makes my heart happy and joyfully sharing my value, but when I reflected and completed the exercises at the end of each chapter, I gained awareness of my emotional disconnects. Thank you for giving me a new lease on life!!

—Ryan Cwick

This delightfully positive, no-nonsense approach to discovering what feeds my soul—and how to value that for myself in all aspects of life—is eye-opening! The stories and fun adventure-positioning make it an enjoyable and impactful read. I'll be buying extra copies for friends, family and coworkers.

—Danielle Seth

If you've ever felt invisible or robbed of personal satisfaction, then this book is for you. The mindful guidance and diverse stories made me feel as if I was not alone. Furthermore, it gave me tools to pursue what—in my heart of hearts—I want.

—Howard Simons

I didn't realize how often I was discounting my own value, let alone my *Heart Value*, before I read this book. There's so much concrete guidance toward and framework for unlocking my value and reclaiming my power based on what matters to me. *Heart Value* is a must-read!

—Erin Bush

This book is a must-read for everyone who feels a void and knows they want something more for their life. *Heart Value* connects readers to their inner truth and gives them the confidence to direct their path according to their heart's desires. Mary Tess demonstrates how to achieve personal fulfillment and joy.

—Brian Gourlay

Absolutely brilliant!! Mary Tess encourages all of us to tap into our hearts to make choices and take action based on our individual priorities and desires. She helps us see that what feels right to us, regardless of external pressures and societal norms, is important to notice and honor.

—Alison Holmlund

The coach in me is excited to see Mary Tess share her expertise, examples and passion to transform lives. *Heart Value* is filled with rich coaching content that is designed to support each reader where they are and where they want to go. I'll be glad to share this book as a resource for those growth-minded people around me.

—Patrick Howe

HEART VALUE

FEEL APPRECIATED IN WAYS THAT MATTER AND DISCOVER YOUR TRUE STRIDE

MARY TESS ROONEY

Heart Value™, True Stride™, Value Vault™ and Activate Appreciation™
are all registered trademarks of Mary Tess Rooney.

Book Cover/Interior/eBook Design by The Book Cover Whisperer:
OpenBookDesign.biz

Interior Graphic Design by Debbie Jarski

Edited by Zoë Bird

Proofread by David Aretha

Library of Congress Control Number: 2021920581

ISBN 978-1-7368609-7-7 Paperback
ISBN 978-1-7368609-0-8 eBook
ISBN 978-1-7368609-3-9 Audiobook

Printed in the United States of America

FIRST EDITION

www.marytessrooney.com

DEDICATION

For my Heart Value relationships

You, my brilliant, beautiful and loving clan of blood and of choice, have blessed my life's adventures. The power of our energetic and emotional connection inspired me to write this book and share this message with others.

Thank you for appreciating my heart, my value, my humor, my spirit and my authentic self. Your constant love, support and laughter fuel my adventures and deepen my awareness of what truly matters.

For the brave, heart-centered souls I have yet to meet

Your Heart Value deserves to shine! I hope you fearlessly choose to surround yourself with a clan, like mine, that ignites more acceptance, understanding, appreciation, kindness and joy in your life. Embrace your Heart Value connections, enjoy your adventures and get your stride on!

CONTENTS

CHAPTER 4: INVEST IN YOUR VALUE VAULT AND RECLAIM YOUR POWER 63

CHAPTER 5: READ THE SIGNS: TRUST YOUR INNER COMPASS 91

CHAPTER 6: PRIORITIZE FUN: ELEVATE YOUR JOY FREQUENCY 107

CHAPTER 7: DIRECT YOUR PATH: CHOOSE YOUR OWN ADVENTURE

CHAPTER 8: DESIGN YOUR EPIC ADVENTURE: ENVISION, PLAN, IMPLEMENT AND CHERISH

FOREWORD

This book is a good read if you want to honor your time and talents, and give based on what truly matters to *you*.

Sometimes you give without expectations because there is a person in need. Other times you share to receive your just reward.

The why, how and with whom you share your value is for only you to decide, but it's important you know the difference and are true to yourself. Or, as Shakespeare wrote in Hamlet: "This above all: to thine own self be true, And it must follow, as the night the day, Thou canst not then be false to any man."

Mary Tess's proud mother,
C. Cullen Rooney

HEART
VALUE

FEEL APPRECIATED IN WAYS THAT MATTER
AND DISCOVER YOUR
TRUE STRIDE

CHAPTER 1

YOUR ADVENTURE BEGINS

Logically, you know that who you are and what you do matters, but there's a voice deep inside you tugging at your heartstrings, reminding you that you want and deserve something more.

Nora was in tears as she retold another upsetting work exchange with her manager. "I think I'm finally ready to resign next week. I can't take this constant stress. I'm outperforming my peers, but my manager doesn't see me… and I'm starting to question my value."

My heart hurt for her. I'd been listening to Nora express the same sentiment—feeling deflated, overlooked and unappreciated—for almost a year now.

Nora continued, "Maybe I'm not as good as I thought I was. Maybe my years of sales experience doesn't matter—maybe everything I do doesn't matter. Maybe, even though I love my job and consistently deliver results, my impact could be greater."

Have you ever felt that way? You work extremely hard to meet expectations and make a difference, but you feel invisible or ignored. You feel stuck and unsure, and your heart longs for *something* more.

What is your *something* that is calling you? Do you long for recognition and kudos because you are a rock star, but hear crickets? Do you crave external validation to quiet the self-doubt brewing in your brain? Do you desire approval—from a loved one, a boss or a peer—to feel like *you* and *your value* matter?

Do you want all of those things, and *something* more? Something that sparks your heart, boosts your energy and brings you joy?

I've been there personally, and I know countless people like you and Nora too. The scenarios might differ, but the underlying theme is the same. You feel powerful in many aspects of your life, but you struggle to follow your heart—to offer value that attracts appreciation, meaningful relationships and joy.

Maybe you feel overlooked or invisible by a loved one or a neighbor instead of a boss. Logically, you know that who you are and what you do matters, but there's that *something* again. A voice deep inside you, tugging at your heartstrings, reminding you that you want *something* and deserve *something* more.

FROM CORPORATE EXECUTIVE TO HEART VALUE™ EXPERT

As a former strategy and communications executive who crafted plans, achieved results and enabled teams' successes, I understand the importance of recognizing talent and impact. There's a magical look in a person or team's eyes when they feel seen, understood and appreciated for a job well done.

On the flip side, it's disheartening when a well-deserving person feels rejected, even though their value warrants accolades. Even worse, it's upsetting to see a gifted individual overlook their own value because they believe that external approval is more valuable than personal satisfaction.

I've experienced disappointment when those who benefited from my value didn't authentically appreciate me. I've gotten so caught up in the hustle and bustle of *doing* that I lost sight of what lights me up. I've minimized my personal priorities—including my health—for the sake of a company's agenda or external approval. I've been so focused on people-pleasing and leading with my head full of expectations that I dismissed my heart's yearning for *something* more.

Let's face it: Regardless of your age or years of experience, you want to feel valued and surrounded by people who treasure you energetically and emotionally. We all do. It's a natural human desire, and a worthy quest.

My natural curiosity—for myself and others—led me to study value and the role it plays in life and relationships. At first, I used my analytical mind to learn about how to feel more valued, fulfilled and connected—until I realized that my *something* and yours has zero to do with logic.

Your heart already knows your *something* intimately. The key is to lead with your heart and trust your feelings to make choices and take actions that align with your *something*. Through my own stories and those of others, like Nora, we will explore ways to unlock your heart-centered value so you can realize more joy, appreciation and meaningful relationships in your life.

YOU ARE THE EXPERT ON YOU

Are you ready to listen to your heart to reveal your *something* and reclaim your power? Are you intrigued by this idea that honoring your value will expose clues that lead you to walk in your truth? Have you reached a point where what's calling you will not be ignored? Are you excited to navigate your adventure based on your dreams and inner compass, to move in the direction you want to go?

If you answered yes to even one of these questions, yippee!! I see you. I understand you (because I've been there). I am here to cheer you on!!

You don't have to feel invisible, deflated and unappreciated for your value anymore. I am thrilled that you are done feeling disconnected, demoralized and perplexed by the lack of *something* in your life. I feel giddy about the fact that you hunger for answers and will not blindly accept society's perception of your value as your truth.

This is *your life*. You are the expert on *you*.

Reclaiming your power and feeling appreciated in ways that matter is more than a logical mission. Your big ol' beautiful heart has precious insights and feedback that will illuminate your *something* as you discover your True Stride™.

Navigating your life's purpose and path by yourself can feel overwhelming, but you are far from alone. In addition to other *Heart Value* readers all over the world, we have True Stride podcast listeners, called Striders, who are on this adventure too.

The Striders' collective offers strength in numbers and shared accountability to support your personal discovery as you get from where you are in this moment to where you want to go. I look forward to walking the talk with you. Together, we will cheer each other on through our highs, inevitable lows and everything in between.

The easiest way to make a commitment to yourself and fellow Striders is to email marytess@truestride.com with the subject line "I'm a Strider." If you know what's calling you, feel free to share your *something* in the body of the email. Or, if you are not yet clear on what's tugging at you, that's okay; just state, "*I am here,* ready and willing to search for my truth and answers."

We accept and cherish you just as you are. The only thing required is your desire to align with your heart in all that you do, so you can feel energized and happy with each step you take. The good news is that by the end of this book, you'll be striding toward your *something* as you implement heart-centered strategies to voice your value and activate more appreciation and joy in your life.

I am honored and eager to join you each step of the way. I am confident that we are going to have an EPIC adventure!!

Before we get going, let's explore the elements you'll find at the end of each chapter. I know starting anything new can be overwhelming at first. Though I'm not there to cheer you on in person, I am with you in spirit, in heart and in these words.

The exercises, tips and questions that follow—if you choose to use them—will empower you to embrace your something and become your own Heart Value expert. My goal is to create a feeling of adventure as you utilize the tools that have helped me and others. The adventurer in me hopes that you are reading *Heart Value* on the beach, at the lake, in a canyon or on a mountaintop—or anywhere that fuels the expansion you seek.

As you read each chapter, I invite you to enjoy the stories, embrace the new ideas and apply the instrumental insights to discover what matters most to you. Some of the concepts might feel easier to adopt than others. Some might feel awkward at first or seem like a stretch, but with each attempt, completion or decision, you will gain valuable insight into who you are, what lights you up and where you want to go.

At the end of each chapter, the exercises—which I call *checkpoints*—allow you to self-reflect so you can take yourself on a *Wise Walk* and *feel, choose and act* with intention. Oh, and you don't have to complete all of the checkpoints. Everyone's journey and needs are unique. I've completed all of the exercises, but I've done so over time and *not* in one sitting.

Here's an overview of the strategies and resources available on your adventure:

- **Checkpoints**: Your chance to take a breather, be present, process and apply the chapter's concepts and lessons to your life. Checkpoints are your opportunity to cherish your aha moments, appreciate how far you've come, acknowledge your expansion, awaken your heart to new possibilities and envision the life you want so you can plan and implement what's next. *Example: What awareness, energies and emotional triggers surfaced as you read this chapter?*

- **Instrumental Insights**: Reminders, takeaways and key messages from the chapter you just read.

- **Wise Walk Reflection**: Heart-centered questions to ground you in your past, present and future. *Example: In this moment, where are you? What feels right and what feels off? What's calling you and tugging at your heartstrings?*

- **Feel-Choose-Act Amplifier**: A self-discovery practice you can use to gauge how your *feelings* influence your *choices* and inform your *actions*. When you understand your heart and head connections, you can intentionally invite more feel-good experiences that align with your *something*. *Example: Nora **felt** deflated and invisible, and craved a meaningful relationship with her manager. Nora made a **choice** to vent to me and consider her options, including resignation. Nora took **action** to stop minimizing her value based on external appreciation, and began to ask different questions to reveal her* something.

- **Affirmation**: Offers a statement in the present tense that you can say out loud or handwrite multiple times to condition your mind and body to manifest your best life.

- **Tip**: Additional support, context or encouragement to get you from where you are to where you want to go!

YOUR ADVENTURE IS UNIQUE...

Remember, you are the expert on you. Since your adventure is unique, you get to decide which checkpoints and reflections are relevant to you. The beauty of this book is that your experience is tailored for you, by you.

I encourage you to read and consider all the opportunities available, but ultimately, only your expectations, rules and desires matter. There's no one-size-fits-all map for you to follow.

Instrumental Insights follow each chapter to reinforce the key messages and takeaways.

Notes:

Instrumental Insights

- Regardless of your age or years of experience, you want to feel valued and surrounded by people who treasure you energetically and emotionally.

- As a *Heart Value* reader—and now Strider—you have joined a powerful collective that offers strength in numbers and shared accountability to support your personal discovery as you get from *you are here* to where you want to go.

- Listening to your big ol' beautiful heart will illuminate your inner truth and joy.

- By the end of this book, you'll be striding toward your *something* as you implement heart-centered strategies to voice your value, Activate Appreciation™ and prioritize more fun in your life.

Affirmation

I lead with my heart. I am aware and experiencing more appreciation and joy in my life.

Tip:

As you read, you'll notice my pattern for naming things. I love language, and I naturally analyze and label ideas, beliefs or methods to quickly recall experiences or sentiments. Naming helps me navigate my own adventure; I name it so I can own it.

Once you embrace our Striders' naming conventions and sayings, your brain will have a shortcut to process, store, recall and apply them in conversation. Don't worry—our new secret language is intuitive, practical and playful. Plus, it gives us Striders a fun common lingo that easily connects with our desired feeling state so we can support each other.

Besides, the branding process—and creating word combinations to trigger comprehension—is fun for me. So I hope you have a laugh each time our common language palette offers an intuitive shortcut.

For example, my podcast and company name, True Stride, inspires a movement where we realize our truth and groove in all that we do. And thanks to my talented book cover and interior designer, Christine Horner, and amazing graphic designer, Debbie Jarski, the visual definitions and illustrations make it easier to recall, enjoy and apply our lingo in your life too.

Get Your Stride On

Your heart already knows your something intimately. The key is to lead with your heart and trust your feelings so you can make choices and take actions that align with your something.

CHAPTER 2

HEART VALUE IN A LAND OF MADE-UP RULES

Before I learned to appreciate my Heart Value, I felt unsupported, stuck, discouraged and sometimes misunderstood—until I realized that I was discounting my own value by giving away my power and allowing others to define my worth.

As I sat in Tiffany's office and stared down at my partial bonus payment statement, I could barely make out my manager's words. She sounded muffled, like one of the "wah wah wah" adults in *Peanuts*, as she attempted to position my reduced annual performance check as a "learning opportunity."

I quickly shifted my eyes from the objectives and key results (OKR) bonus document to her face so I could fully process her bewildering message.

"Overall, you will receive 90 percent of your OKR bonus," Tiffany said. "I had to submit a zero attainment for your Customer Toolkit goal, which accounted for 10 percent…because, unfortunately, you did not get that deliverable 'to market' as you stated."

"But Tiffany, it's done," I replied. "I handed it to you and the leadership team signed off on the final deliverable. Everything is ready to execute. The customer-facing documents, communications, frequently asked questions and more. How can you ding my paycheck when my part was completed? I executed what was expected of me. Management delayed the launch because the business wasn't ready yet."

"As your manager, part of my role is to teach you the importance of language, and in your OKR, which *you* wrote, you said, 'Craft, prepare, plan and bring Customer Toolkit to market.' I realize you did everything in your power, so this isn't a reflection of your final comprehensive deliverable or your thoughtful efforts…but as a company leader and steward, I'd be doing you a disservice if I didn't teach you to be more accurate in how you articulate your OKRs. Let this be a lesson for the future."

I was miffed. I wasn't making a ton of money, so I'm sure 10 percent of my overall bonus seemed like peanuts to her, but I couldn't believe she was using her authority to "teach me a lesson" based on her interpretation of the company's made-up rules.

I'm a highly driven Virgo who is strategic, collaborative and detail-oriented, which meant my customer-facing materials, backed by diverse, brilliant subject matter experts, was a masterpiece (if I may say so myself). To not receive a financial reward for that business goal because of a technicality that Tiffany chose to exploit was bullshite. She robbed me of money that I had legitimately earned, and stripped me of emotional satisfaction in a job well done.

Of course, I was also heartbroken. Tiffany used the company's "*at your manager's discretion*" fine print to assert her power arbitrarily. Her lesson wasn't empowering. It was demotivating.

Not only did I feel unseen for my value, I felt unappreciated. This was not my first lesson in the importance of value and appreciation in my life, nor would it be my last.

If you relate to my story of receiving less than you deserved—or deserve—financially and emotionally, I'm sorry. Denigrating a person's value and impact based on made-up rules is unacceptable, and you deserve better.

If you struggle to relate because you don't receive a compensation bonus, then consider a time when you were overlooked for a promotion, passed over for an award or had your contributions ignored. At that moment, did you feel invisible? Did you begin to question your value or wonder why you didn't feel appreciated?

As humans, we crave meaningful connection at work, at home and in our community. We have an innate need to feel seen, heard, understood and appreciated for who we are and the value we offer that lights us up.

This realization ignited my passion to help individuals rise above office politics to get promoted, recognized and rewarded. And that ultimately evolved into a deeper exploration of *seeing* my own value, *feeling* appreciated in ways that matter, and helping others do the same.

PROMOTE YOUR WORTH AND PUT IT IN THE PAYCHECK

Lily, an import/export sales executive, was distraught when she called me one evening because her annual bonus was not commensurate with her performance, impact and value.

Months prior to the bonus payout, Lily and her president/boss, Marvin, had had candid conversations about the challenges she faced and overcame with only one employee, Sally, to assist her. Marvin was removed from the day-to-day demands, so he lacked insight into Lily's management of client relationships to retain and grow revenue for the company.

Lily and Sally had collaborated strategically and intensely to win back a disgruntled client, which prevented a multimillion-dollar gap in revenue for Marvin's business. Since they got paid based on the company's overall revenue, Lily made the solid case that this challenging situation did not impact the company's bottom line and therefore Sally deserved a higher bonus. Lily stated her case factually and compellingly. The good news was that, when bonus day arrived, Sally's bonus reflected her efforts to save that high-dollar client.

However, the bonus Lily received did not reflect *her* value, leadership and efforts. She had successfully managed and maintained a client relationship whose loss would have been devastating if she and Sally hadn't salvaged it. She knew her talents and contributions, but her missed opportunity to communicate her value resulted in less money and a bruised ego. She certainly did not feel appreciated. Lily was hurt. She felt frustrated that she had wrongly assumed her successful advocacy for Sally's bonus increase meant that Marvin would automatically recognize the correlation between Sally's value and Lily's value.

We've all been there. We've assumed that our value and leadership would be recognized and rewarded. Yet our silence leads to missed opportunities to promote our worth and increase our paychecks.

Advocating for Sally, her employee, made Lily a great manager and leader; but unfortunately, she unintentionally discounted her own value by not highlighting her own contributions and worth. Lily needed to advocate for herself in addition to Sally. The headline should have read, "Lily and Sally saved the company millions of dollars and secured a long-lasting relationship with a formerly disgruntled customer."

How many times have you provided accolades for one of your team members while secretly hoping the audience would make the connection to your own value? You shy away from asserting yourself because it can be perceived as tacky or boastful, and yet

MARY TESS ROONEY

you secretly *hope* that someone's paying attention and that your actions will speak loudly enough for you to be compensated for your efforts.

According to Ashley Stahl's 2016 Forbes.com article "How Self-Worth Affects Your Salary,"[1] research has shown time and time again that people with higher self-worth have higher salaries.

It's not surprising. If you value what you have to offer, you will make sure you're rewarded for your contributions.

Don't wait for someone else to notice your strengths or how you contribute and make a difference. Recognize the full worth of your value and raise the price for what you offer. Admire and respect your value enough that others hold your value in high regard and put it in the paycheck!

MEMORABLE MIDNIGHT RIDERS

We can point to examples throughout history where the *documentation* of a person's value was essential to their getting the credit they deserved.

Most Americans probably recognize the name Paul Revere. He was the midnight rider who warned his countrymen on April 18, 1775 that the British were coming. Would it surprise you to learn that there were four other courageous Boston patriots who also rode through towns on horseback to sound the alarm that the Revolutionary War had begun? Their names were William Dawes, Samuel Prescott, Israel Bissell and Sybil Ludington.

All five riders—Paul, William, Samuel, Israel and Sybil—successfully completed their mission.

William rode south while Paul and Samuel rode north. Israel rode for over four days, completing 365 miles. Sybil, a brave sixteen-year-old female rider, covered over forty miles (double Paul's ride) on April 26 to warn Connecticut colonists that the British were coming.

The towns they alerted were similar, so why does Paul's value to our great nation live on—centuries later—while William, Samuel, Israel and Sybil are barely known?

In 1775, social media and outlets for breaking news did not exist. But Paul wrote a detailed first-person account of his ride. He had a strong network and was active in his community, so, without knowing it, he acted as his own publicist.

In contrast, very few records of the rides made by William, Samuel, Israel and Sybil exist. They did not *document* their brave deeds or make an effort to share them, so Paul got all the credit by default.

I find this story illuminating because well-deserving individuals get overlooked and ignored all the time.

How many times have you been the most talented person in the room, one who just made a significant impact, but found that the attention was directed at someone with less skill or value? In that moment, did you wonder: *Why am I invisible?*

What can we learn from Paul's actions? What can we learn from the *inaction* of William, Samuel, Israel and Sybil?

We learn that your notable contributions are your story to tell, and it's your responsibility to share your value if you want to stand out and get the credit you deserve. What actions can you take to promote yourself and be more like Paul?

LEARN FROM THE LIMELIGHT-LOVERS

Peter was an extremely competent training director, and he owned it. He made it a priority to remind his team, peers and executives of his skills. Peter never missed an opportunity to promote his own contributions, and he often used humor to toot his own horn. After a boastful rant highlighting his impact, he'd follow up with, "But let's be clear, I am confident, not cocky."

Some found Peter's peacock-like behavior a little off-putting, but I respected his self-confidence and unapologetic self-praise. Looking back now, I see that he was ahead of the curve. He was proud and outspoken, and he never got ignored or overlooked. He loved what he did and bravely advocated for his right to feel seen and recognized on a continual basis.

Inga, an operations leader, was eager to earn awards and fame to elevate her reputation. As such, she instructed her team to scour the company, the industry and relevant organizations for upcoming awards and submit nominations on her behalf. At the time, I judged her and viewed her plan as self-serving and a poor use of company resources because it was focused on her own agenda. Now I realize it was pure marketing genius. She saw the benefit of plastering her name and agenda within related communities to raise her brand, gain credibility, expand her following and increase her influence.

No one knew that, behind the scenes, her team was the submission engine fueling her continuous presence in the limelight. Nor did they care that she was sometimes prioritizing those awards and accolades above mission-critical company directives. That wasn't noteworthy. What mattered was public recognition of Inga's name, picture and accolades. This made her appear award-worthy and advanced her career.

Harlo, a marketing leader, craved the limelight too. He cleverly put himself in every video message internally produced at his company because he understood that if thousands of employees continually saw his face and heard him interviewing the executive team about company directives, his reputation would soar. Harlo became memorable, and as he strategically inserted himself into major initiatives, a perception surfaced that he was at the heart of all of them. Again, I disapproved of this self-serving tactic at first. But upon reflection, I understand that it's brilliant marketing.

Let's face it, whether it's 1775 or the present day, recognition is prevalent among individuals who *invest* in their own value and readily shine the light on themselves. They are so attuned to their Heart Value that they willingly work the room, navigate

> **Heart Value** is your energetic and emotional connection to the value you offer that lights you up.

politics and put themselves first. Peter, Inga and Harlo all exuded confidence and created memorable opportunities to stand out, regardless of their skills or acknowledgment of others who may have played key roles.

Stop judging the proud limelight-cravers. Instead, get curious and learn from them! Confidence is contagious and personal power begins with *you*.

WHAT IS HEART VALUE?

In everyday conversations, a person's value is often measured by external standards. If your value is useful and unique, and others have come to rely on what you offer, then your value is perceived to be high. If the value you offer is not in demand or useful to others, then your value is deemed to be low by external standards.

Society encourages us to assess an individual's value based on what others think. We commonly hear sentences like, "Mary offers a lot of value on this topic; make sure she's a part of this decision-making process." Or, "Howard's experience is valuable; what does he think?" Or, "Let's include Veronica; she adds so much value to everything we do." Or, "If we want to get this right, Ryan should lead this effort."

This idea of evaluating the value you offer based on others' opinions is so common that we begin to judge ourselves based on external conversations and requests to be of service or included. It's always nice to feel needed or wanted, but I never hear anyone say, "Mary offers a lot of value on this topic. If this topic lights her up, make sure she's a part of this decision-making process." Which is a shame, because your relationship with the value you offer is far more important than what anyone else thinks.

My friend Mac was a gifted baseball player. Game after game, Mac was the most valuable player (MVP). His high school talent earned him a college baseball scholarship. While in college, he had enough talent to get selected by a Major League Baseball professional team in the draft. But Mac didn't enjoy playing the game.

He used his MVP pitcher status to earn a tuition-free business degree, and good for him. Mac knew in his heart of hearts that he would not be happy playing in the pros. Baseball was fun for him as a kid, but after his freshman year in high school, he completely lost interest in the sport and found no personal fulfillment in playing or winning MVP status. As a sophomore in high school, he lost his Heart Value connection—and yet he went on playing for seven more years because he didn't want to disappoint anyone and was enticed by the financial rewards he could gain from sharing what others valued in him.

Most likely, we can all relate to Mac on some level. We prioritize external incentives—like societal pressures, kudos or financial rewards—over our own personal fulfillment. But are you using that value exchange as a phase to get closer to what you really want? How long will trading your happiness for what others find valuable in you be acceptable?

Heart Value is *your* understanding—on a cellular level—of who you are and what lights you up, and how that synergistically connects with others. You get to decide how to channel it to live your best life. Honoring your Heart Value gives you clues to follow your heart, walk in your truth and move in the direction *you* want to go.

No two people are alike. The value you offer is distinctly unique and extremely powerful when it comes from your heart and benefits the right audience.

I'd bet money that there are contributions you offer that make you feel amazing.

Perhaps not everyone "gets" or "appreciates" your value, but their perspective doesn't make *your value* less treasured.

I love the rush I feel when my natural talents and passions align, and when recipients see, understand and appreciate my value and its impact. When I'm out of alignment, my inner light dims and my energy suffers.

I'd venture to guess that you too have an inner light that shines brightly or dims based on the value you share and who it serves. If you stop to reflect, you might admit that when you deliver value to please others, or because it's expected, you feel drained afterwards.

Whether you know it or not, your Heart Value affects how you make choices, interact with people and derive fulfillment from this world. When you are fully connected to your Heart Value, you will realize increased confidence, visibility, earning potential and joy.

And yes, the term Heart Value may feel new to you, as it did to me at first, but the more you embrace and use it, the easier and more intuitive it'll feel. This language of our heart inspires us to want *something* more for ourselves. Even people who struggle with anything new expressed feeling more energized and emotionally connected after they overcame their initial resistance and started to use "Heart Value."

ACTIONS SPEAK LOUDER THAN WORDS

I grew up in a large Irish Catholic family that valued modesty and humility. My mother, who is known for her pithy one-liners, continually reinforced the idea that "actions speak louder than words." As one of thirty-six first cousins (on Mom's side) this made a ton of sense to me. Can you imagine what our family parties would be like if all thirty-six kids made a practice of talking about themselves? All bragging or boasting about how great they are in their unique way? Yuck, as Grandma would say.

Instead, we were encouraged to demonstrate our value, but never speak of it. We grew up with the guidance that we should allow our hard work and individual gifts to "speak for themselves." In my family, it was impolite, crass or arrogant to "toot your own horn." There was almost nothing worse than "lip service." Oh, the horror!

This value system accompanied me in all of my endeavors—school, work, sports, games and extracurricular activities. Looking back, I believe it is a generational or cultural thing. You were considered a "class act" if you were modest about your talents or accomplishments. Don't pat yourself on the back. Work hard and, once you've earned it, others will recognize you for it. This philosophy was true for my family, and perhaps it's true for you too.

Throughout the majority of my career, I was too humble or too busy to promote myself. I relied on the graciousness of others to draw attention to my strengths. Or, if I was asked to compile a highlight reel of my accomplishments, I usually gave my team credit instead. I elevated the "team" efforts, even though I alone was responsible for the "team's" success or failure.

Fortunately, as I began my career, most of my bosses adhered to this same philosophy. They thought it was cute that while I had extremely high drive and successfully conquered any problem, I didn't seek the spotlight.

They too were raised to assess value through actions, not words, so my career steadily progressed without my having to promote myself. I bought into a system that said that if I worked hard and showed results, I would be recognized and rewarded. For many years, that approach worked, in spite of my inability to appreciate my own Heart Value.

Fast-forward a decade, and I began to see this practice crumble. The rules had changed without notice.

I witnessed peers who tastelessly "tooted their own horn" getting promoted and celebrated instead of being seen as boastful. I repeatedly watched talented and well-deserving individuals get overlooked, ignored or outmaneuvered by more aggressive and better-networked colleagues. I noticed a massive rise of vocal leaders who, instead of being perceived as arrogant or conceited, were rewarded and recognized as experts based on their repetitive talk track or marketing tactics.

At first, accepting this behavior as the new norm was painful. Those of us from the humble generations were taught that self-promotion was tacky and redirecting praise or commending others was classy.

I took pride in being "classy," so initially, I resented the heck out of those apparent outliers who weren't playing by the same made-up rules. I missed the memo that said, "WARNING: socially acceptable norms have evolved, and your hard work will seem *invisible* if you don't speak up."

And I learned I wasn't the only one who had missed that memo. Many of my friends and colleagues experienced similar frustration. Of course, emails have replaced memos, so perhaps that was part of the problem (ha!). Regardless, many of us were trying to get a handle on how to adapt and thrive in our new surroundings. I wonder if you can relate to some of the issues that surfaced for us.

- Have you ever had to escape to the bathroom, fighting back emotions (like frustration, anger or tears) because you were rejected for something you were overqualified for?

- At this stage of your life, do you want to be known as classy—or appreciated for the value you offer?

- When have you felt frustrated because your value was overshadowed by self-promoting individuals similar to Peter, Inga and Harlo?

- If you were given strategies to increase your confidence, visibility, earning potential and joy, would you commit to making your value a priority?

MARY TESS ROONEY

- Are you angry or embarrassed when you think back to times when you or others diminished or drowned out your value?

- Can you recall a specific time you downplayed your value or redirected credit or praise for accomplishments toward others? How would you insert your value in the conversation now, knowing you have to be your own biggest champion?

I bet you (or someone you know) can relate to these sentiments and desires. When I think back to my first aha moment regarding this sea change, I thought, "Crap, you invested in being known as classy, not in the value you offer." Does classy pay the bills or help others connect to the expansive person I am? No.

Over the years, I've noticed a major shift in how leaders, companies and individuals recognize and reward value. It's no longer a game of actions alone that gets you the credit you deserve. It's a game of voice your value or risk getting overlooked, misunderstood or misaligned with *what matters* most to *you*.

In my core, I still believe that actions speak louder than words. You have to "walk the talk" in order to be credible and gain respect. And, when you follow up those actions with clear and compelling self-promotion that is authentically and uniquely you, you drive home what differentiates you, what you value, what you want more of and how the world benefits from your unique gifts. Who doesn't want that?

WHAT HOLDS YOU BACK

In this day and age, there are a number of reasons that can muddle your effectiveness when it comes to expressing your value, such as limiting beliefs, generational viewpoints, a frantic pace, external pressures, societal norms, technological advancements and emotional challenges. Have you too been hindered, for one reason or another, in clearly understanding your value?

In part, this is because everyone is inundated with messages that vie for attention. It's also partly because technology and social media have devalued modesty and humility. And the sad reality is that we can be tough on ourselves. This critical mind-chatter minimizes your Heart Value and impact.

Imagine if you protected and honored your Heart Value as you would for a dear friend. The shift in vibration is huge.

Consequences of Not Knowing Your Heart Value	Benefits of Knowing Your Heart Value
~ Use your strengths to people-please and benefit others, but derive little joy or satisfaction from them yourself	~ Gain clarity on what makes you uniquely you
~ Feel disconnected from your inner compass, as well as audiences that appreciate you for the things you do enjoy	~ Increase confidence and self-worth
	~ Tap into personal insights about what brings you fulfillment, joy and happiness
~ Get distracted by others who pull you in different directions that serve and benefit them, not you	~ Consciously choose how to live life and plot out future goals and plans for how to move forward
~ Forget what brings you joy at your core	~ Choose your people and the company you keep (who you hang out with)

MARY TESS ROONEY

~ Lose sight of your personal goals and your vision for a joyous life	~ Gain grounding framework in difficult or stressful times; move through conflicts or challenges with greater ease

If you struggle to honor your Heart Value, you may be feeling deflated, unappreciated, disconnected or disregarded because of your own experiences of getting overlooked, ignored or outmaneuvered based on made-up rules.

You are not alone.

Before I learned to appreciate my Heart Value, I felt unsupported, stuck, discouraged and sometimes misunderstood. Then I realized that I was discounting my own value by giving away my power and allowing others to define my worth.

The land of made-up rules no longer resonates with my heart center or inner compass. My heart, mind, body, energy and soul desire to adventure beyond the limited and political constructs of made-up rules that once seemed acceptable and important.

As soon as I committed to living my adventure, according to *my own rules*, a massive energetic shift occurred. I unlocked the power of my Heart Value, and learned how to use it as a means of exchange so I could connect with genuine appreciation.

CHECKPOINT: YOU ARE HERE

I love those maps in amusement parks and nature trails that visually indicate, *You are here.* The checkpoints and Wise Walk reflections contained throughout this book serve to help you identify your starting point so you can discover your path to unlocking more joy, appreciation and meaningful relationships in your life.

You are here for a reason. Get clear on your "why" and invest your time, energy and effort in the exercises that speak to you. Don't judge your "why." Hold it in your heart to motivate you to enjoy *your* adventure, at *your* pace and with *your* goals in mind.

Remember, there are a million ways to explore the checkpoints at the end of each chapter! As you select interesting, fun or inspirational ones, you can meander, walk,

MARY TESS ROONEY

jog or sprint down these many trails and paths. There are no rules or expectations, only your inner compass to follow in pursuit of your *something* so you can enjoy the life you are being called to live, one checkpoint, one self-reflection and one experience at a time.

Instrumental Insights

- Diminishing a person's value and impact based on made-up rules is unacceptable.

- Honoring your Heart Value gives you clues to help you follow your heart, walk in your truth and move in the direction *you* want to go.

- When your Heart Value is out of alignment, your inner light dims and your energy suffers.

- When you are fully connected to your Heart Value, you will realize increased confidence, visibility, earning potential and joy.

- Get curious and learn from the proud limelight-cravers. Confidence is contagious and personal power begins with you.

- Made-up rules are just that. You are the authority on your life.

- As soon as you commit to living your adventure according to your own rules, an energetic shift will occur.

- Unlock the power of your Heart Value, and use it as a means of exchange so you can connect with genuine appreciation.

Wise Walks are your opportunity to slow down, check your reality and ask questions to gauge your energetic and emotional responses. Each heart-centered *feeling* provides clues that influence your *choices* and inform your *actions*.

Notes:

Wise Walks are your opportunity to slow down, check your reality and discover what heart-centered *feelings* align with your *something*. Take your time to review the Wise Walk Reflection questions and process your heartfelt answers. Journal without judgment and let your thoughts flow freely to walk in your truth and move in the direction you want to go.

1. Identify one area in your life where you feel unappreciated, overlooked or ignored for your value. What *feelings* surface and what feels off? What is limiting you—your own thoughts and limiting beliefs, or living by made-up rules?

2. List one or more past decisions that didn't help you feel valued or understood. Knowing what you know now, what choices would you make differently? What new *choices* do you need to make to overcome limiting beliefs or obstacles?

3. Starting today, what's one *action*, however small, you can start taking in your life to move in the direction you want to go?

FEEL-CHOOSE-ACT AMPLIFIER INTRODUCTION

Since this is the first time the **Feel-Choose-Act Amplifier** appears, here's additional context. This is your opportunity to apply the chapter's concepts and lessons to your life. Reading about my or someone else's struggle and awakening might trigger an aha moment in you, which is awesome. But if you want to experience your own awakening, it's helpful to take your insight one step further and correlate it with your relevant example to make a long-lasting impact. This is your resource, so feel free to use an example from your past, present or future to become more intentional about the direction you want to take.

- ~ **Feel**—In the *feel* section, list what emotions surfaced for you as you read this chapter. Be present with your thoughts, observations and reactions to understand what is true for you. Noticing where you are aligned or unaligned is powerful.

- ~ **Choose**—In the *choose* section, consider your options, listen to your heart-based feelings and document or make your choice. Don't stress. The good news is, you'll always have the ability to choose again. Based on your feeling information, you have the ability to explore your possible choices and create a go-forward strategy. There are several trails and off-the-beaten-paths available to you if you take the time to evaluate the possibilities.

The **Feel-Choose-Act Amplifier** is a self-discovery practice to notice how your *feelings* influence your *choices* and inform your *actions*. When you understand heart and head connections, you can intentionally invite more feel-good experiences that align with your *something*.

Notes:

Which paths feel right for you are based on how you want to feel and what you want as a result.

~ **Act**—Once you are clear on your feelings and choices, it's time to take action. Commit to steps, however small, to move you in the direction you want to go. You will gain momentum with each step you take. And remember, you can always stop, change direction or take a detour if something feels off. As time goes on, your actions will come from a place of inspiration, which will foster exciting results that align with your True Stride.

FEEL-CHOOSE-ACT AMPLIFIER

Observe an area in your life that you'd like to address and apply this *feel, choose and act* amplifier. Jump right in, or read the following examples to get your Feel-Choose-Act juices flowing.

Feel	Choose	Act

Feel ▶ Choose ▶ Act

Feel	Choose	Act
I felt unappreciated working for Tiffany, and angry and hurt that the company's made-up rules affected my paycheck.	I couldn't change Tiffany or the company's managerial discretion policy, but I made a choice to own my value and tell my story. I also made a choice to seek out and surround myself with people who did appreciate me.	I developed an action plan to help me clearly understand Tiffany's expectations. I began documenting my value. And I started an internal job search because, while I loved the work I was doing, I wanted to work for someone who would protect my Heart Value and give me the credit I deserved.
Lily felt frustrated and disappointed that her boss, Marvin, didn't increase her bonus based on her actions alone.	Lily chose to acknowledge that she should have included herself in the headline and advocated for herself, in addition to Sally.	Lily met with Marvin to voice her value, and Marvin provided a second bonus payment to account for Lily's efforts in saving the client.

Affirmation

I deserve to feel appreciated for my value,
and I make choices to voice my value and
take action to surround myself with
Heart Value relationships.

Tip:

If you feel stuck or unsure where to start, begin with an introspective
activity (walk, paint, take a bath, etc.) to create movement, check
your current reality and release any blocks that are weighing you
down. Introspective activities get your awareness juices pumping.
Movement creates a shift of energies that allows new perspectives
and ideas to flow so that journaling and creating thoughtful
action plans become easier.

Notes:

Get Your Stride On

Your notable contributions are your story to tell, and it's your responsibility to share your value if you want to stand out and get the credit you deserve.

Endnotes

1   Ashley Stahl, "How Self-Worth Affects Your Salary," Forbes.
com, May 11, 2016, https://www.forbes.com/sites/ashleystahl/2016/05/11/
how-self-worth-affects-your-salary/?sh=243006de77fa

CHAPTER 3

VALUE AND APPRECIATION SWEET SPOT: FINDING YOUR TRUE STRIDE

I am the reward administrator for my own life, and I consciously choose who benefits from it.

Most learning and development departments end each training program with a survey requesting feedback on the course objectives, delivery and application to trainees' everyday responsibilities. In my first year as a corporate sales trainer, I recall tallying the results for a weeklong training I had conducted and preparing to review them with my manager, Taylor. I was nervous about sharing the results with Taylor because, out of one hundred respondents, one individual gave my speaker style an "okay" and another gave me a "dissatisfied." To my surprise, Taylor was very complimentary. He praised my effective content delivery and audience engagement and provided a lot of recognition for a job well done.

When he asked me if I had questions or comments, I promptly pointed out that two of the participants did not give me glowing reviews.

Taylor chuckled and asked, "Do you honestly expect to please everyone all of the time?"

I had not expected this question or his laughter. I replied, "Don't you expect me to read the audience and ensure that I meet their needs?"

Taylor looked shocked and disheartened as he said, "Mary Tess, out of one hundred participants, ninety-eight raved about you and the entire program. Ninety-eight individuals listened to you for a full five days and said it was one of the best trainings they've ever attended and how excited they were to get back to the office to apply what they learned. Ninety-eight percent had only positive things to share and comment about, and yet you are focused on the two percent—well, really only one percent—who didn't appreciate your 'speaker style.' But even they validated the importance of obtaining the necessary learning objectives in order to do their jobs effectively. Do you realize that, based on these results, you are focused on the wrong feedback?"

I was taken aback. He was right. I was beating myself up for two participants versus the overwhelmingly positive responses of the other ninety-eight.

What's interesting is that all one hundred attendees, plus Taylor, valued the job I had done and learned what they needed to be successful in their roles. The only thing missing was that *I* didn't feel appreciated by two individuals who didn't completely align with my "speaker style." I'm not even sure what "speaker style" means, but Taylor and I suspected it meant they didn't appreciate my direct, fast-talking New York approach and dry sense of humor, which Taylor compassionately reminded me is what makes me, *me*.

Furthermore, the only way I got ninety-eight percent to see *and* appreciate my value was by being my real self. Taylor explained that in teaching, training and leading, trust is essential. The only way to establish trust is through vulnerable authenticity.

Since the vast majority clicked with my authentic self, why was my attention disproportionally directed at the outliers? Why is it that we humans tend to believe and focus on the negative rather than the positive?

Sure, it was easier for Taylor to have emotional distance and perspective from these results; they were not criticizing or commending him. And there it is again—I unconsciously placed the term "criticizing" before "commending" as I wrote that sentence (ouch!). Sadly, we are hardwired to place a negative value on our flaws, but we shouldn't overlook heartfelt praise because it's critical in helping us increase our confidence and elevate our worth. What we focus on becomes our reality. Let me repeat that: What we focus on becomes our reality.

Even though I was true to myself and delivered the content authentically, I briefly allowed the two percent to get into my head and question my value and unique offering. In that moment, I lacked confidence—and I didn't understand the difference between *validation* and *appreciation*. I now know that validation confirms that what I did mattered. I had an impact and, based

Validation means that your value is desired and makes an impact. **Appreciation** confirms that you are sharing your value with the right audience, one that has an energetic and emotional connection to you.

Notes:

on survey results, all one hundred participants validated that they had obtained the required learning objectives.

Appreciation is a synergistic alignment of energies and emotion. Appreciation calls into question whether I was serving the right audience and if we established a mutual symbiotic connection.

In this case, an overwhelming ninety-eight percent appreciated the value I offered; but as my career progressed, this delineation between *validation* and *appreciation* would continue to surface.

Thank goodness Taylor was competent and reframed the results for me, because I loved that job. Training and teaching fueled me. I felt energized, appreciated and encouraged to share my unique gifts and style, and I impacted thousands upon thousands more learners as the years went on.

Are there instances when you minimize your value because you place too much importance on negative perceptions versus overall positive feedback? How do you plan to adopt the behavior of intentionally focusing on what's right, instead of what's wrong, in your life? Are you prepared to repeat this mindful shift until it feels natural and becomes your norm?

In what areas of your life do you feel completely appreciated? Recall a time when you felt a genuine emotional connection with an individual, team or group. What was it about that experience, specifically, that gave you a sense of synergistic alignment? Did they express gratitude for your Heart Value?

ADVOCATE FOR APPRECIATION

Michael, a tenured leader who possessed an abundance of institutional knowledge, heart and critical thinking, was my trusted advisor. Even though we worked in different departments, I often included him in meetings to brainstorm opportunities, expose weaknesses and strategize around initiatives to implement for the betterment of our employees and customers.

I valued Michael's unique perspective and appreciated his ability to articulate potential pitfalls before we got too far down any one path. Contrary to leaders who surround themselves with yes-men, I invited devil's advocates like Michael to meetings. I valued complete information, including knowing what wouldn't work, more than validation that an idea was good. The approach that stemmed from this belief system encouraged diverse thinkers to speak up and present unpopular ideas, or point out red flags related to my projects so the team could make informed decisions.

Michael's troubleshooting mindset resulted in a more thoughtful strategy and approach. If he was on board with a direction, I had more confidence it would work. He saw every potential breakdown and wasn't afraid to voice his concerns. He made the team better by considering all angles, and he made me a better leader because I could set direction based on more comprehensive and complete insights.

While I appreciated Michael's gifts, not everyone on my team felt the same way. Disgruntled team members would come to me with their complaints. Their general comments were "he slows us down" or "he pokes holes in everything we are trying to do."

I would explain my genuine appreciation for his unique attributes. Some open-minded individuals would validate that his experience, understanding and passions mattered. Others were too closed off and could only see the challenge his presence posed to their workload.

I reframed the conversation so that others could learn to appreciate—or, at a minimum, validate—that his expansive value earned him a seat at the table. In those moments, and unbeknownst to Michael, I was his public relations (PR) agent. In time, my team began to see how his thought process improved their understanding, output and decision-making skills before we got too far down any one path.

In my position of authority, I could advocate for Michael's value with my team. He had knowledge, candor and perspective that no one else could duplicate. I didn't want that to go unnoticed because I appreciated him.

Some employees understood his rare value on an analytical level and validated the fact that his contrarian mindset upped our game, but still diminished his value behind the scenes. More often than not, insecure employees couldn't emotionally connect to Michael. Perhaps they felt threatened by his ability to raise potential breakdowns early on, which meant they needed to think through and anticipate risks as they presented possible solutions.

Regardless of their opinion, I knew Michael was extremely valuable. I was happy to promote his gifts within my sphere of influence and, as a result, he attracted additional appreciation from individuals that greatly benefited his career.

Ultimately, Michael and I deeply appreciated each other's Heart Value. Our work relationship thrived because we saw how our energies and emotions aligned. We accomplished tons together and each cared for the other as a whole person—mind, body, spirit and soul.

Together, our inner light shined much brighter, and man, we shared many memorable laughs. To this day, I love how our support of each other's energies created the freedom for us to be ourselves and operate in a safe, synergistic environment.

Who is the Michael in your life? With that person in mind, what have you noticed about your free-flowing exchange of energies, laughter and appreciation that empowers you to offer value that matters to you? Have you told your Michael how much you appreciate him, her or them?

We all deserve to have our Heart Value soar. Who is acting as your PR agent? If you don't currently have one voicing your value behind the scenes, make a list of potential advocates and continue to nurture that mutually beneficial relationship. If you do have one, connect with them regularly to ensure that they know what lights you up and have a trove of sound bites ready to showcase the Heart Value that matters most to *you*.

VALUE UNIQUE OVER SAME

As young children, some of us grew up with encouragement to "be more like Jane." (Substitute whatever name or names apply.) Our parents' innate protective nature coached us to successfully assimilate in a world that *values sameness*. They were not always conscious of doing this, but can you blame parents for wanting to protect their kids from criticism and bullies by encouraging them to just *blend in*?

Valuing unique attributes in a world that emphasizes conformity and sameness is challenging. This is true for us as children, and it's true for adults, too.

Acceptance and appreciation for an individual's *unique* talents and gifts are equally rare in corporate America. Many corporations still use standard "performance management" reviews in an attempt to level the playing field while distributing annual performance ratings and merit increases; however, the language used to measure an employee's performance usually has subjective, objective and quantifiable components.

A manager's assessment can either build you up or knock you down, and managers are not typically trained to evaluate without a bias lens. If your boss is emotionally connected to your Heart Value, you will probably receive appreciation for a job well done. If they are not emotionally invested in your value, the best you can hope for is validation for meeting expectations. And if they don't see your value, well, then…you either have to work extremely hard to become visible, find a new boss or discover a new earning opportunity, because lack of acknowledgment for your worth wears you down emotionally, physically, spiritually and mentally.

> A **superpower** is a unique talent or ability that makes a valuable impact.

> **Notes:**

Driving the awareness of your unique importance, worth and usefulness in this world is vital. That energy emits a frequency to the collective relationships in your home, workplace, community and the world at large.

While owning your authentic power is critical for your own self-worth, appreciation is a natural human need that reaffirms your impact based on the value you offer. Others are more likely to reinforce that and become your advocates, whether you're in the room or not, if you authentically own and amplify your own value attributes.

When you honor your own authenticity and proudly amplify your gifts, your self-respect and admiration shine through. In meetings, Michael would sense outside disapproval or pushback when he acted as devil's advocate. It didn't go unnoticed, but Michael was mature and confident enough to know that contrarian thinking is one of his superpowers.

He wasn't going to dim his superpower because it made a few uncomfortable. That was their issue and insecurity. And thank God he resisted their negative energy, because I saw and connected with his gift, which allowed me to happily act as his PR agent. Eventually, he won some over—and even the ones he didn't click with validated that the team's deliverables benefited from his unique perspective.

GO FOR THE GOLD

As a manager, my favorite question to ask in interviews was, "If

MARY TESS ROONEY

the business world adopted Olympic-style events to honor outstanding performance, for what business skill would you take home the gold?" If the applicant had a totally perplexed look on their face, I'd offer, "For example, I'd win the gold in managing large, complex, cross-functional and diverse teams. I'm gifted at sensing an individual's potential, talents and strengths. I excel at empowering each team member to use their unique gifts to achieve business goals, help establish a collective voice and gain personal successes. I believe that if everyone plays to their 'gold medal' passions, diverse teams emerge that deliver solid results on time and within budget."

I asked this question for three primary reasons. One, is the applicant self-aware enough to know what top business event would win them the gold? Do they revel in a specialized area like data analytics, which to me is akin to synchronized swimming for its precise movements and scoring? Or do they comment that they are a generalist in their respective discipline? Two, the Olympics requires heart, commitment and talent. Depending on their answer, I'd discover if they were connected to what lights them up at work, and if they have the ability to lead with their heart. Three, I'd get a sense of whether they prefer to work on solo projects or on a team.

There was never a wrong answer. I asked because I was curious to learn more about the potential candidate beyond traditional interview questions. And over more than two decades, my Olympic gold medal inquiry helped me build successful, energetically thriving, fun-loving teams, comprised of both direct and indirect coworkers. I loved working with diverse teams of high-energy people who were dedicated to getting stuff done.

What is your Olympic gold medal event? Is it one of your superpowers? How often do you share it with others? Make a list of individuals or groups who love to watch you in action or benefit from the value you offer. Generally speaking, the ones who seem energized to receive or witness your superpower are also the ones who appreciate your Heart Value. Strive to spend more time with them.

DON'T LET NEGATIVE NITWITS DRAG YOU DOWN

While working in corporate America, I had a disgruntled employee, Cruella, who, despite my best efforts to build a gold medal team, decided to place judgment on me for *her* unhappiness. Unbeknownst to me, she documented any perceived flaws in my leadership and then spread her negativity to the other team members, human resources and even the company's "Report It!" hotline.

I say "perceived" because her claims were false and unsubstantiated. Cruella and I *never* had an adult, transparent or productive conversation about her opinions. Instead, the company assigned an investigator, Loki, who lacked integrity, objectivity and the professional training to conduct a fair investigation.

When Loki interviewed me (supposedly to hear my side of the story), it was clear he had already drawn a conclusion. Interviewing me seemed more like a box to check than an exploration of facts to ensure a safe and healthy work environment for my team and me.

Loki's questions were leading and had zero to do with performance. He made biased, blanket statements like, "I've spoken to *everyone* on the team, and they all said that on occasion you have tone."

I questioned, "Everyone? You spoke to everyone on my team and they all said I have 'tone'?"

"Yes, everyone is in agreement," he replied.

This came as a shock because I had team members who worked

MARY TESS ROONEY

for me for ages and followed me from role to role. They raved about my leadership style, support and ability to champion their success. I was also shocked because my recent annual employee satisfaction scores and personal development indicator (PDI) assessment results illustrated extremely positive and complimentary feedback on my leadership. Per the company's tools and credible PDI framework, one hundred percent of my employees (everyone participated) stated that they valued my leadership skills, abilities and style. I didn't score average, let alone below average, in *any* area.

After a long, pregnant pause, I attempted to clarify with Loki. "You spoke to David... Jessica...Betsy...on my team and they *all* said that I have tone?" As I was about to name several other team members, Loki interrupted. "Well, I didn't speak to them."

"So how can you say 'everyone' when you haven't spoken to my entire team? And do you intend to speak with my entire team to gather a complete picture of my style before you make these broad statements that impact my reputation?"

"Who I interview is at my discretion. So, is there anything you'd like to say about your tone as a leader?" Loki asked.

"I'm an extremely caring, thoughtful and respectful leader. I work hard to support, encourage and lead my team. Can you provide me with an example or specific incident when my tone was in question?"

"I don't have any specific incident, but again, everyone feels you have tone," Loki reiterated.

I was literally speechless. How were we back to "everyone" when we had just established that Loki hadn't spoken to *all* of my employees? He could not cite one specific example to substantiate the claim and seemed to be cherry-picking people based on a stacked deck.

I share this story with you because this incident was one of the catalysts that inspired me to evaluate the correlation between honoring my value and feeling appreciated by those who sincerely matter. I learned that my Heart Value deserves to shine. People may try to dim my light, but that's only possible if I let them.

Bullies and negative nitwits like Cruella and Loki may try to judge you—using unsupported information and flawed, made-up rules—but their perception doesn't define *you* or *your value* as long as you don't let it. Zoom out, evaluate the big picture and be sure to give as much credence to those who truly *value all of you*, including your tone (ha!)—if you have one.

For a time, I kept analyzing this unbalanced investigation, which felt akin to a modern-day witch trial. Thankfully, Ariel, a dear friend, said, "Mary Tess, please stop. Bullies are not emotionally evolved. You operate at a much higher frequency than oppressors so you will never understand their mindset. Each time you seek to fathom their mentality, you lower your frequency to their level. The more you try to relate to them, the more their negative energy invades and damages yours."

Whoa! She was right. Each time I recalled the disappointment I experienced with that unfair and painful memory, I lowered my naturally positive frequency.

As with my post-training survey expansion experience, I had the opportunity to acknowledge the energetic and emotional appreciation I received from the majority versus the few. If I wanted to elevate my frequency, I needed to shift my focus to high-vibration individuals who aligned with my vibrant energy, and could see *and* appreciate my value.

In Masaru Emoto's book *The Hidden Messages in Water*[2], he used years of scientific research and photography to illustrate the effects of a person's thoughts, feelings and words on water. In his studies, the influence of positive and negative energy on water's purity, structure and ice crystal formation were evident.

When water was spoken to with love and gratitude, its crystals were fully formed and beautiful; while negative words of harm or misery created dark, incomplete or nonexistent crystals.

MARY TESS ROONEY

Humans, who are mostly water, are affected by energies and our environment too. In his book, Emoto states, "All things vibrate, and they vibrate at their own frequencies." He gives an example: "A person experiencing great sadness will emit a sadness frequency, and someone who is always joyful and living life fully will emit a corresponding frequency."

From time to time, we all encounter a Cruella or a Loki. The key is to not lower your energetic or emotional state to their level, which only weighs you down. You have too much to offer that is appreciated by others. Focus your energy on individuals who match your frequency and appreciate your value, and enjoy feeling lifted up and empowered to offer more.

AWARDS-SMASHING

Most organizations place a high emphasis on praise, awards, accolades and public recognition. In partnership with two savvy executives, I even created a quarterly and annual recognition program for anyone in support roles who contributed to a sale. A ton of work is required to secure, transact and bill a sale, so this program allowed individuals and teams to receive credit for their contributions too. In addition to monetary recognition, they received faux crystal awards to proudly display in their offices or cubicles.

Over the course of my career, I earned many crystal, glass and metal trophies that represented my outstanding contributions and exceptional impact. For me, those awards represented more than what I'd done for the business and company. They symbolized nights, weekends and other priorities that took a back seat so I could be *valued* and *appreciated* at work. Let's face it, an opportunity cost comes with every achievement. More often than not, there is a personal loss behind every company accolade.

In Marie Kondo's book *The Life-Changing Magic of Tidying Up*[3], Marie guides readers to declutter their homes using a category-by-category focus. She challenges them to hold each item in their hand to determine if it should stay in the home or be donated, "and ask: Does this spark joy? If it does, keep it. If not, dispose of it." Thank it for its service and place it in the donation pile.

When I held my awards in my hands, they did not spark joy. Instead, I had a deep sense of sadness and some regret as I vividly recalled what I had sacrificed, endured and postponed for the sake of the company's agenda. Those reflections made me cringe. Even worse, I once again realized the impactful misalignment of validation versus appreciation. I also noticed that my emotional response depended on *who* had presented me with an award. Some objects surfaced hollow, empty approval, while others vibrated warmth for me as a human in addition to my noteworthy contributions.

As I charted my new path, I realized that I didn't want awards to weigh me down or clutter my clarity—so I decided to smash them. The preparation was tricky, since I wanted to avoid leaving any shards of glass on my patio or in my driveway depending on my smash site. After much deliberation, I selected my driveway because I cared more for my sweet German shepherd, Cali, than I did my truck's tires. My neighbors had already witnessed me doing some odd things around the 'hood, so I figured, "What's one more thing for them to talk about?"

In the early morning hours, I laid out several cut trash bags and double-wrapped each award in a gallon-size Ziploc® bag. Then I held each award overhead—as if it were a soccer ball and I was preparing for a sideline throw-in—and then relished the CRASH as each one hit the cement driveway! The real crystal mementos produced a crisp sound as they shattered into a million little pieces, which was very satisfying. The glass ones made more of a thud as they fractured to a lesser degree, but both kinds of smashes sparked joy. I laughed heartily from both the absurdity and emotional release as I placed the remains in my trash bin. Mission accomplished.

Perhaps it seems a bit dramatic (heh heh), but it was a cathartic gesture that symbolized my freedom from made-up rules and external limitations. It's easy to get caught

MARY TESS ROONEY

up in wanting to stand out and know that our work and efforts matter. However, it's unbelievably freeing once we decide to define our own value. I am the reward administrator for my own life, and I consciously choose who benefits from it.

In an unexpected way, smashing my past accolades created a literal *break* of matter that set my mind free. The award release fragmented the physical matter, which opened space for new mind matter—of my own choosing and design—to take shape.

Now, I surround myself with individuals who truly appreciate me and my worth. I soak up and savor daily small wins, impressive fails and everything in between. I confidently embrace all experiences as an accrual of value. I am quick to say *yes* to moments that bring me joy, and *no* to people and situations that deplete me. I proactively set goals and reward systems to recognize my gifts, impact and growth.

As you move through life, how much power will you give the external world when it comes to defining your own value? For those of you who know your value, do you also know—in your heart of hearts—whether you are surrounding yourself with people who validate your value? Are you connected to people who truly appreciate not just what you accomplish, but what you miss as a result of the time, energy and resources you sacrifice to get the job done?

Your value is easy to see, honor and display based on tangible examples and compelling results. What's harder is gaining clarity on your emotional connection to sharing your value (how it makes you feel). Does offering your value make you proud or make you cringe? Do you feel validated or appreciated by those who benefit from your worth? Are you devaluing yourself because you are surrounded by colleagues and peers who aren't emotionally invested in your overall well-being?

FINDING MY TRUE STRIDE

As a child, I avoided running. I was active, athletic and competitive, but I generally chose sports and their respective positions by the least amount of running required. In soccer, I was the goalie. In softball, the catcher. When I had to choose between field hockey and volleyball, well...I played volleyball.

Maybe I was intimidated by the scrutiny associated with running. If I embraced running, would I ever be fast enough? Growing up, I remember friends getting teased because their gait or movements were awkward, like Woodchopper Betty. I had already endured the freckle-face, carrottop and Mary Mary Quite Contrary nicknames, so I was not looking to attract additional attention.

While I was athletic, my running pace was slow and steady, so I didn't purposefully opt into running until college. My focus was on fitness, not fun. This was the first time I had not played a sport in school and, of course, I had indulged too much at the dining hall and after hours. The freshman fifteen were filling out my baggy jeans in short order.

The first time I hit the streets was painful. I struggled with my pace, mind chatter and breath. I had to mentally fight a barrage of excuses, but I knew running was my best path to being able to button my formerly baggy jeans (no joke).

My mom's voice in my head motivated me to put on my sneakers and get out the door: "Show up, and let God do the rest." I kept showing up and, before I knew it, I was a runner. Not a fast one. I wasn't going to win any medals, but I witnessed a transformation that included benefits to my body, stress levels, mindfulness, energy, confidence and so much more.

I was living in Manhattan's Lower East Side, and running helped me quiet the noise and expectations that buzzed around me. It was my solo time to connect with myself. No headphones, music or distractions. Just me. My thoughts. My breath. My sensations. My forward movement.

I loathed the first ten minutes of the run, but by minute eleven, my endorphins kicked in, my breath steadied, my pace hit a groove and my mind calmed. Amidst a bustling world of chaos, running made me feel better. Dare I say, it even brought me joy.

I experienced a love affair with that feeling of rhythmic connection, inner confidence and forward movement. It wasn't the act of running itself that kept me logging miles. I simply enjoyed that feeling of alignment, power, peace, strength and like-minded connection with other active, good-natured individuals.

Solo running provided *my mind* with a safe space to *be* with and evaluate my *feelings*, *choices* and *actions*. *My body* responded positively to my engaged muscles, increased heart rate, controlled breath and pulsing pace. *My soul* elevated as I hit my meditative stride and found my groove. *My heart* always felt lighter, happier and more peacefully aligned after I finished a run.

Runs with friends or group runs offered deep, soulful conversations and connections that were heartfelt, supportive, encouraging, comical and real. I've maintained lifelong, genuine bonds thanks to this act of consistently hitting the pavement. I've formed meaningful friendships with runners I first randomly encountered at the New York University campus, Central Park, work, races, parties and training events who shared my desire to experience the benefits and effects of running.

As I continued to run, my goal-oriented personality prompted me to join the New York Road Runners Club and I completed countless races, two marathons and many fun runs. I rarely ran for competitive reasons, but I loved the camaraderie and unwavering support I found amongst runners regardless of anyone's speed, size, shape, ethnicity, gender, sexual orientation, profession, etc. Races, especially in Central Park and surrounding areas, were a big melting pot and the common bond was a genuine appreciation for fellow runners looking to find their *True Stride*.

Each runner has their own unique True Stride. Generally, runners are a happy,

Notes:

grounded and supportive group. Honestly, I haven't met many negative nitwits who love the benefits gained from running. I suspect the consistent practice of creating a safe space for self-care, self-reflection, endorphin boosts, a sense of accomplishment and happiness is our own reward.

Finding your True Stride is a metaphor for trusting your inner compass, directing your life, setting your pace, overcoming resistance, honoring your rare essence and expressing your value to rhythmically move forward in whatever activity energizes and fuels you. This metaphor extends far beyond running and is applicable whether you are an artist, manager, business owner, writer, student, baker, parent, juggler, photographer, teacher or athlete or engage in any other pursuit that ignites your Heart Value.

When it comes to knowing your value, how much weight do you give to external acknowledgment versus internal satisfaction? How much does your inner voice guide you on your path, versus external voices?

When you think about discovering your True Stride, ask yourself: What is akin to running in your life in that it offers you an internal knowing to trust your rhythm, flow and transformation? For me, running is a release. It restores balance and offers me healing, light, growth, laughter, love and a supportive community. How are you tuning into your feelings and channeling them to move forward in an optimal, connected, aligned way?

As you hit your True Stride, do you *feel* energetically and emotionally connected with the right audience? Where in your

MARY TESS ROONEY

life do you see a delineation of validation versus appreciation? Are you running your own race, your way, or do you try to keep pace with someone who merely validates the value you offer?

People of all genders are told not to *feel* or *share* emotion, but that's bad advice. Your feelings provide powerful clues to what lights you up and makes your heart happy.

Don't dismiss your feelings or desires. Focus on where you want to go and how that makes you feel. What's the predominant feeling you want to create in your life?

When you are clear on what you want, you can break the bad, externally based patterns and negative thoughts that hold you back more readily. It's clarity about what feeling you are running toward (not away from) that enables you to find your True Stride.

Remember, there's only one person you are accountable for, and that is *you*. You deserve to be aligned with your True Stride and feel that euphoric state throughout your life. It's time to follow and lead with your heart.

My experiences with high-vibration individuals like Michael, Taylor and Ariel versus negative nitwits like Cruella and Loki made me realize the power of my thoughts, feelings and words on my own frequency. My self-talk and the company I keep have the ability to raise me up or weigh me down, if I let them.

The more I honored my value and my high vibration, the more my heart, mind, body, spirit and soul moved forward in a fluid and frictionless way that I call True Stride. This discovery set me on a path to match the value I offer with those who genuinely

Joy Frequency refers to the level at which your vibration radiates harmony and blissful energy, inward and outward. Your goal is to have a high amount and occurrence of joy felt in your life, which means you consistently do things that light you up.

Notes:

appreciate my entire being—in my truest authentic form—which ultimately raised my joy frequency.

What began as a journey to own and promote my value (and empower others to do the same) evolved into a more meaningful awareness of the sacred relationship between a person's value, how it makes them feel, and how they energetically and emotionally connect with others.

CHECKPOINT: FIND YOUR TRUE STRIDE

As you reflect, notice your emotional responses. Each heart-centered feeling that surfaces provides clues that will influence your choices and inform your actions.

Instrumental Insights

- ~ Don't minimize your value by placing more weight on negative perceptions than overall positive results.

- ~ Validation and appreciation are distinctly different.

- ~ When your Heart Value is aligned with another person, your combined energies fuel the freedom to be yourselves and operate in a safe, synergistic environment.

- ~ Voicing your value is easier with a behind-the-scenes public relations (PR) agent who advocates for your Heart Value.

- ~ Seeing value based on examples and results is easy. What's harder is finding clarity on your emotional connection to sharing your value and how it makes you feel energetically.

WISE WALK REFLECTION

Journal without judgment and process these Wise Walk questions to gain awareness. Let your thoughts, feelings, choices and actions flow as a stream of consciousness.

1. What feelings surface when you think about negative feedback or negative nitwits in your life? When you share your Olympic gold medal event (what lights you up), what is your body's physical response? How do you feel when you are aligned with your True Stride?

2. If your Olympic gold medal event or superpower creates a high, what choices will empower you to feel this and use your gifts more? What past decisions helped you discover your True Stride, and can you apply similar choices today? Sometimes, what's worked in the past will act as a springboard to move you forward. For example, if an exercise or morning routine worked for you in the past, that's a proof point worth exploring. If you are stuck, what new choices do you need to make to overcome limiting beliefs or obstacles?

3. Starting today, what's one action, however small, that you can start or stop doing to align with your True Stride, feel appreciated and move in the direction you want to go?

FEEL-CHOOSE-ACT AMPLIFIER

Observe an area in your life that you'd like to address and apply this feel, choose and act amplifier. Jump right in, or read the following examples to get your Feel-Choose-Act juices flowing.

Feel	Choose	Act

Feel	Choose	Act
I felt genuine appreciation for Michael's gold medal superpower of articulating potential pitfalls before we got too far down one path.	I chose to advocate for him as his PR agent because I understood the importance of finding his value and appreciation sweet spot.	I always invited him to meetings and continually reframed conversations behind the scenes to give others the opportunity to learn to appreciate, or at minimum validate, his expansive value.

MARY TESS ROONEY

Affirmation

I prioritize positive feelings and
people in my life. My choices
and actions honor my value. I
am surrounded by people who
energetically and emotionally
support the superpower that
lights me up.

Tip:

The more you self-reflect, honor your feelings, evaluate your choices
and take decisive action, the more you will realize your True Stride.
If you want to make strides and gain momentum in the areas that
matter most, surround yourself with supportive people. Their energy
and encouragement will make the impossible feel possible.

Notes:

Get Your Stride On

Question made-up rules with discernment.
Play the game your way, according to
your rules, and create a mindful shift from
external expectations to internal knowing.

Endnotes

2   Masaru Emoto, *The Hidden Messages in Water* (Hillsboro, OR: Beyond Words Publishing, 2001), pp. 41-42.

3   Marie Kondo, *The Life-Changing Magic of Tidying Up* (New York: Ten Speed Press, 2014), p. 41.

CHAPTER 4

INVEST IN YOUR VALUE VAULT AND RECLAIM YOUR POWER

When I saw my professional accomplishments neatly categorized in black and white, I was flooded with concrete evidence, emotional reflections and an intense awareness that deepened my appreciation for my own impact on this world.

Working for Sachiel, my manager, as a communications leader was fulfilling, stimulating and rewarding. He was a brilliant, savvy and caring leader who conscientiously protected the company, employees, customers and shareholders.

During a one-on-one meeting, Sachiel asked me to provide a comprehensive overview of what my team and I had produced and communicated to drive revenue and employee engagement over the past year. This seemed like an odd request at first, since he was extremely aware of every deliverable—until I realized that my overview would be exhibited in front of other executives. I suspected he was preparing for a political storm (from which he graciously spared me) and was planning to fight with facts. I was thankful that Sachiel took it upon himself to appreciate my Heart Value and act as my PR agent.

My small but fierce team began combing through our monthly reports and organizing projects by category. We created an executive summary for each initiative and compiled tangible examples, compelling results and meaningful metrics. We offered Sachiel an electronic file with embedded multimedia hyperlinks and a graphics-rich binder to illustrate our contributions and impact.

It was a comprehensive body of work, and we appreciated Sachiel's Heart Value, too, so we were determined to use this opportunity to showcase his direction as well as our work. His leadership and support empowered us to execute projects, avoid time-consuming political agendas and ultimately improve the company's bottom line. It seemed right that we make him proud to tout our accomplishments and the value we delivered under his oversight.

Sachiel beamed with pride when I delivered our twelve-month dossier. He was grateful for our thoroughness because it easily justified our value and thwarted the covert political attack he sensed was brewing.

I was thankful he was astute enough to proactively advocate for us. The additional benefit was the pride my team and I felt when we saw our impactful value in a tangible, accessible, measurable and data-rich form.

From Paul Revere, we learned that your notable contributions are your story to tell, and that it's your responsibility to share your value if you want to stand out and get the credit you deserve. In this example—like Paul—we presented a firsthand account of our ride. We included all notable riders, their roles and our collective post-ride outcomes in our account. That body of work was personally and professionally satisfying because it increased our confidence, visibility and worth.

Too often, in our haste to respond to constant business demands, we forget to document our story and celebrate our achievements. At Sachiel's request, we made voicing our value a priority. This was fulfilling, rewarding and a worthy investment.

Finding your True Stride is much easier when you consistently tell your story. You are more than a one-hit wonder.

Sadly, I wouldn't implement a consistent practice of reflecting, documenting and sharing my achievements until years later. Sachiel didn't require it to see my value, so I put my energies elsewhere.

CHANGE OF LEADERSHIP, CHANGE OF POWER

Not needing to be in the spotlight is one thing, but shying away from praise because you don't care about center stage is another. For a good portion of my career, I was happy to remain in the shadows of leaders I respected. I was not an attention-seeker. But the rules work against you if your successes are not widely understood or appreciated.

After my amazing run working for Sachiel, I acquired a new boss, Alfie. He validated my value, but I quickly realized he was not going to advocate for me like Sachiel did. Alfie and I didn't have an energetic or emotional connection. He was too consumed by management changes and prioritizing his own agenda to concern himself with my visibility.

His focus was on managing up, not down. I'm sure you've had a similar experience. One boss makes you feel valued and appreciated. The next boss makes you feel invisible or strictly in service to making them look good.

Add a change of leadership power or direction, and all sorts of questionable behaviors surface. When new leaders come onto the corporate scene, I've witnessed behaviors that could pass for untelevised versions of the TV show *Survivor*[A], where people jockey for positions and form alliances (including secret alliances) to stay in favor.

I worked hard to avoid political games; I'm too honest and empathetic to participate. But I was savvy enough to know that without Sachiel, I had no PR agent and was at risk of getting ignored, overlooked or voted off the island.

Realizing my compromising position, I brainstormed ways to advocate for myself and become more visible without having to jockey like the rest of them. The easiest option was to solicit outward recognition. An industry award would get me on the radar and publicize my major contributions and successes.

During a one-on-one with Alfie, I boldly asked him to nominate me for an industry award that was relevant, applicable and appropriate. I had spent a lifetime helping other people gain recognition and rewards for their successes, so I was intimately aware of the process, protocol and expectations. I more than met the criteria, so I had nothing to lose.

Unfortunately, Alfie, who was probably feeling vulnerable too, politely denied my request. When I asked him what I needed to do to be considered, he replied, "You need to document your accomplishments."

Yowza!

I was disappointed and stunned. Did I know I was valuable? Absolutely. Did Alfie know I was valuable? Absa-fricken-lutely.

Was he going to advocate for me? Nope. Was this another *sign* that I needed to become my own champion and PR agent? Yes.

Reading the signs finally motivated me to prioritize my own Heart Value so I could feel appreciated in ways that mattered. I went on a mission to document, affirm and invest in what I now call my "Value Vault™."

MARY TESS ROONEY

WHAT IS A VALUE VAULT?

Your Value Vault is an account of all the physical, mental and emotional experiences that have made you, *you*. Your Value Vault holds your treasured successes, your impressive fails and everything in between, including how each experience made you *feel*.

When I began this exercise, I was focused on not missing out on an award, but I quickly realized that I was thinking too small. What I learned from my twelve-month dossier created for Sachiel was the importance of taking stock of my professional accomplishments in order to advocate for my worth and ignite personal satisfaction. If I could do it for one twelve-month period, why not think bigger and do it for my entire career? It brought to mind another one of Mom's wise sayings: "Anything worth doing is worth doing well."

Your **Value Vault** is an account of all the experiences—your successes, whoopsies and everything in between—that have increased your value and made you, *you* (including how each experience makes you *feel)*.

Notes:

This heightened awareness meant capturing my past and present. Fueled by a desire to honor my value and get the credit I deserved, I scoured decades of files to document my value. In some ways it wasn't all that fun, but this act of collecting, organizing and displaying my value—in my Value Vault—was the best gift I ever gave myself.

I'm extremely visual, so I started with a career timeline beginning with my first paid gig for babysitting at age thirteen. I wanted to consider all of my roles and responsibilities, and make sure I didn't overlook any value I gained from the exceptional performance I consistently delivered. My timeline continued: beach security guard, lifeguard, waitress, intern on ABC's *One Life to Live*…and the list went on.

Once I completed my career timeline, I decided to work backwards, starting with my most recent role. For each position, I started with my annual goals and achievements. These were low-hanging fruit for which I already had descriptions and documented results.

If you work in a company or a small business that doesn't require annual performance objectives, consider starting to do this for yourself. You don't need anyone else's approval or validation to invest in your Value Vault. Documented clarity on your goals will empower you to affirm and better communicate your expansive value. You are worth taking the time to make this a priority.

Admittedly, after I compiled decades' worth of proof points in one document, I got a little overwhelmed. I knew that implementing a discipline similar to my twelve-month dossier would be beneficial, but my bright idea to include and organize *all* of my career highlights seemed daunting.

When the magnitude of this task started to alarm me, I enlisted the help of a friend and thoughtful PR professional, Raven, to help me assess and summarize my Value Vault. Again, I could hear Mom's wise words: "Many hands make light work."

Throughout my career, I've believed in the buddy system as a great tool for keeping forward movement going. Investing in my Value Vault, which spanned my lifetime,

MARY TESS ROONEY

seemed an enormous task. I had hit a productivity wall and needed to make my goal of completion seem more accessible, or I'd risk abandoning a worthwhile objective. I was not afraid to ask for help, and the fabulous Raven was an amazing partner in affirming and summarizing my value.

This was my story to tell, so I still had to do the heavy lifting and oversight. I culled my archives of congratulatory notes and emails to compile my tangible examples, compelling results and meaningful metrics. Raven was at the ready to help me objectively create an executive summary.

It wasn't fancy. I had no intention of sharing my Value Vault with anyone else. I merely wanted to make honoring my value a priority. Also, I knew that if I went through the trouble of documenting all of my past contributions, dating back to my childhood, I'd continually update my Value Vault because I had no intention of repeating this time-consuming activity.

It's important to note that, as I created my Value Vault, I experienced four challenges that were unique to me.

One, I didn't know anyone who had done this, or attempted to dive deep into their past accolades and growth in such a way before. I was a midlife pioneer when I decided that my Value Vault was a critical investment in increasing my confidence, visibility, earning potential and joy.

My better-late-than-never dossier of accomplishments contained a lot of information to organize into digestible headlines and newsworthy stories. Everyone wants messages to be succinct and relevant. If I'd been acting as my own PR agent throughout my career, or had someone's example to follow, it would have been easier to condense my value into key messages. Thankfully, this process helped me distill my highlights down to eight pages of simple and impressive results.

You have the benefit of my learning curve. Because you are reading this book, you now have access to me and others who have invested in their Value Vaults. Their stories will inspire you to create your own Value Vault using my template or your own framework.

Two, while it was personally satisfying to see my impact on the businesses, communities and leaders that I had served, I almost missed events that I'd led in addition to my "day jobs." For example, I oversaw, organized and managed community events for more than five hundred people in New York City. This was no small feat, but I made it look easy. Multiple examples surfaced that weren't necessarily part of my day jobs, but clearly made me award-worthy. Since I'd found meaning and personal satisfaction in doing them, I hadn't looked for public recognition. The big question I found myself asking was, "Why settle for personal satisfaction when you can easily add public recognition?" They can coexist.

In what areas in your life have you accepted personal satisfaction as the reward? Are you great at something, but minimize its impact because it feels effortless? What value do you offer that also brings you joy? Are you ready to share your gifts and feel appreciated? It's time we realize that Heart Value and appreciation can coexist. They are not mutually exclusive, and you deserve to appreciate your Heart Value that brings you joy.

Three, if I had started investing in my Value Vault and preparing to voice my value earlier in life, this process would not have been as arduous. With my guidance and support, individuals in their early twenties find this exercise easy. The reality is, the older you are, the more value you offer, which means this exercise will literally take longer.

If you sense that investing in your Value Vault will benefit you, what are you waiting for? The longer you wait to invest in your Value Vault, the more you'll have to gather, organize and summarize. Regardless of your age, treat your value as an investment and put it in your vault.

Four, I was compelled to do it, but at the time, I had no evidence to demonstrate how investing in my Value Vault would dramatically change my life for the better—which, of

MARY TESS ROONEY

course, it did in spades. When I saw my professional accomplishments neatly categorized in black and white, I was flooded with emotional reflections and an intense awareness that deepened my appreciation for my own impact on this world. I had an accessible reference to promote my worth.

The evidence was concrete, and the results were tangible: what I did made a difference. My Value Vault awakened me, and was far more significant than any crystal award, accolade or promotion could ever be.

After my coaching clients share their Value Vaults, I witness positive behavior and perception shifts, such as increased confidence and pride. Whether consciously or not, they've reclaimed their power. They have a deeper awareness of their value and their desire to feel appreciated in ways that matter. You have the ability to experience this shift, too. Invest in your Value Vault and take a step toward discovering your True Stride.

INVEST IN YOUR VALUE VAULT

You already have amazing achievements, compelling examples and meaningful results that showcase your value, so what are you waiting for? It's time to document your value consistently and in a way that is easily repeatable, memorable and fun.

Have you had a boss who appreciated your Heart Value and acted as your PR agent? Did you make a consistent practice of raising your reputation even though they saw your value?

Imagine the increased confidence, the satisfaction you'd feel and the visibility you'd benefit from if you compiled your tangible examples and compelling stories daily or weekly. What actions are you willing to take today to make your notable contributions a priority?

Regardless of your age, motivation or job, this act of collecting and organizing your accomplishments in your Value Vault is enlightening. Your value becomes more visible, memorable and appreciated. And you enjoy the personal satisfaction and increased confidence from seeing your value come to life on the page. Get help if you need it, and write it. Own it. Celebrate it.

With your PR advocate hat on, identify your motivations for investing your time, attention and energy on elevating your reputation and brand. Are you seeking career advancement, an award, a pat on the back or personal satisfaction? What's driving you to invest in your Value Vault and fuel your proactive PR campaign?

LEARN ALL YOU CAN: IT'S MONEY IN THE BANK

From a young age, I was taught to value learning. Every morning, our school sendoff included Mom's wise words, "Learn all you can; it's money in the bank."

I have a deeper appreciation of that adage now. Every experience, lesson, success, failure, relationship and interaction is an accrual of value.

My mother emphasized the importance of continuing to invest in ourselves, because once you have knowledge, no one can take it from you, and with each deposit, your value grows.

My three sisters and I thrived on this guidance. We understood the importance of owning every experience—yes, the good, the bad and the ugly—to increase our development and worth. Since we were also raised to value modesty, we rarely tooted our own horns; but we knew our strengths and we didn't fear failure. Failure, in our household, was necessary to grow. "Learning is living," Momma still says.

As I reviewed my Value Vault, which was comprehensive in terms of job-related endeavors, I realized that I was selling myself short. Professional accomplishments were only one aspect of my expansive value. I was indirectly giving my power away by allowing societal norms of career identity to define my worth.

Too often, we look for big, defining moments to showcase our value. Or we look for approval from others for what is deemed valuable in the land of made-up rules. Or we think that people only value what happens during the workday, so we dismiss little moments in our personal lives that are meaningful too.

The old definition of value allows others to determine our worth. As I began to reclaim my power by investing in my Value Vault, a new definition empowered me to place value on each experience, to treasure and share them as I see fit. With or without external validation, my value is a collection of all my experiences: professional, personal, emotional, physical and spiritual.

Through every positive, negative, neutral, life-changing and challenging experience, we become more of who we are and were meant to be. Each small interaction creates an imprint we carry with us to the next opportunity and moment.

In my forties, I see my life as a series of experiences that fueled my growth. Some big wins, some difficult losses, some complicated situations and some downright ugly circumstances have all contributed to the human I am today. What I've grown to appreciate is that, as we age, we are constantly gaining value.

Each interaction and growing pain increases my value. It's not just the corporate kudos, sports achievements or academic awards I won that define me. It's the emotional awareness I gained as a result of each "expansion experience."

EXPANSION EXPERIENCES

An "expansion experience" is a moment, interaction or milestone that increases your value. These expansion experiences—whether professional accomplishments, personal achievements, hurtful hiccups, entertaining encounters, comical crossroads or devastating detours—are your story to tell, in whatever creative format you choose to share. The act of courageously telling your story leads to increased confidence, visibility and appreciation (which we all need and long for).

You are far more expansive than what you "do" to support your lifestyle. Bad, hurtful or negative experiences give you a means for comparison and an opportunity to want something more or something different. If everything were good all of the time, there would be no reason for expansion.

You are constantly gaining value. With age, your expansion experiences and value stack up. Don't forget to be like Paul Revere and write a first-person account of all of it!

And yes, when I talk about *expansion experiences*, I mean that this is your chance to include the really hard, uncomfortable stuff—the situations that hurt your heart, that you'd rather not think about, but can't deny helped you grow. As a result of each challenge, you grow stronger, more compassionate and more deeply connected to and aware of who you are and where you want to go.

From my expansion experiences of miscarriage and divorce, I gained extreme empathy. From my cancer diagnosis, I have a unique understanding of managing complex health situations, facing mortality fears while remaining optimistic and making tough decisions when all routes seem less than ideal. From my efforts to write this book, I have rediscovered my voice, learned to be more vulnerable, released old limiting beliefs, connected with brilliant authors and made new friends—and the list continues to grow.

What's exciting is that every experience deepened my ability to find my True Stride, and offer great empathy, rich perspective and extensive kindness. We all long for human connection. We

MARY TESS ROONEY

want to know that we matter, that our highs and lows, our triumphs and defeats, are not for nothing.

When you honor all of your life experiences and are willing to be more vulnerable with them, true human connection and *expansion* happen. You never know who, from your inner circle or the wider world, may share a similar experience.

My friend Connor married a lovely woman, Grace, who was kind but shy and standoffish, especially compared to our boisterous group of childhood friends. At gatherings, she'd fade into the background, and I often wondered if she didn't like us or just couldn't get a word in edgewise amongst the gregarious personalities.

Before our mutual friend Billy's fortieth birthday bash, Connor disclosed that he and Grace had suffered a miscarriage. As Connor's friend, I was able to be there for him, but I didn't feel close enough to call Grace and offer her my condolences.

At Billy's party, I had a brief moment alone with Grace to tell her, "I'm so sorry for your loss. I had a miscarriage at eleven weeks, and I have a deep appreciation for your pain and heartache. Let me know if you need anything or ever want to talk, about anything."

Grace hugged me like never before as her raw and candid emotions flowed. This exchange lasted only minutes, and yet our relationship and the group dynamic changed, in a positive way, forever.

Grace and I are not best friends, but our shared vulnerability bonded us. She's no longer standoffish or content to sit on the sidelines. Now, she's genuinely more amused by the group banter and confidently zings a few witty retorts when we gather. Perhaps our brief conversation allowed her to feel seen as her independent self, not just Connor's wife.

Our shared tragedy allowed me to see the power of expansion experiences. Before our exchange, I viewed my miscarriage as a grave loss. Because I'm an eternal optimist, my brave heart wanted to find a positive aspect to that loss. I wanted to believe that "what does not break us makes us stronger," but my grief overpowered my ability to see growth.

I still know what I lost, but I also see how my Heart Value expanded from that loss. I gained empathy, sensitivity, compassion, perspective and courage. I recognized how important it is to make myself emotionally available if my own pain can support someone who is grief-stricken and suffering from dreams unmet.

We learn from our disappointments and hardships. There is power in pain. So, as you invest in your Value Vault, don't limit yourself to only your professional accomplishments and personal achievements. Document your expansion experiences as well. You are richer from all of the paths you've journeyed. Take time to see, understand and appreciate how your expansion experiences have enriched your Heart Value.

EMOTIONAL CONTRAST

I said it before, but it's worth saying again: Your value is easy to see, honor and display based on tangible examples and compelling results. What's harder is gaining clarity about your emotional connection to sharing your value: how it makes you *feel*.

My Value Vault, complete with professional accomplishments, personal achievements and expansion experiences, unlocked new awareness and clarity for me. Honoring and displaying each experience gave me emotional insight.

If you are visual, like me, think of each Value Vault entry as a gem or precious metal that can be securely treasured in your Value Vault. As I observed each gem, I found myself asking, "How does this experience make me *feel*?"

MARY TESS ROONEY

I realized that, to walk in my True Stride, I had to surface feelings that aligned with my Heart Value, or didn't.

With each reflection, the *emotional contrast* that appeared was jarring. Some of my contributions gave me a joyous sense of pride and satisfaction, while others made me cringe as I remembered with pain what I sacrificed, postponed or endured for the sake of the company's agenda.

Notes:

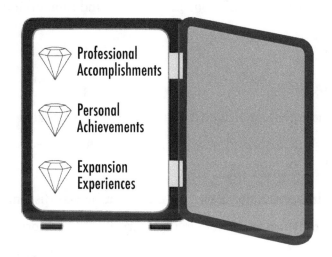

I was surprised by some of my reactions. Some things at which I excelled, and others valued, I dreaded. I love helping, serving and empowering others, but not at the expense of my own happiness. One of my Achilles' heels is people-pleasing, so taking time to self-reflect with each memory gave me a safe space to evaluate what energized me and fueled my soul.

It was helpful to ask myself, "Who benefits from my super-power, and how does that exchange make me feel? Do I share my gifts with people who validate my value or truly appreciate me?" I began to note the positive gems and True Stride experiences so I could chart the gifts I wanted to repeat.

When I gave myself permission to listen to my inner compass, not others, I reconnected to what mattered to me. The deeper connection to my Heart Value served as a steadfast guidepost.

Can you recall a recent exchange that provided you with greater empathy or capacity for kindness, a broader perspective or knowledge that you didn't possess before? How have your experiences made you connect with your Heart Value and humankind on a deeper, more fulfilling level?

ROCKY, SOPHIE AND DANNY

Rocky, a clever, competent and affable manager in his late thirties, struggled to find a fulfilling career path. His résumé displayed new roles every one to two years, which made him appear fickle, suspect or undesirable.

While those adjectives didn't accurately depict his character, he was disconnected from how to discover his True Stride and leverage it to earn money. Unfortunately, he had gotten into a pattern of giving a company a year of service; if he determined it wasn't a long-term fit, he'd move to a different industry. This pattern prompted interview questions related to his frequent role changes. Those questions, while valid, began to erode his confidence.

When Rocky presented his Value Vault, a four-page, bulleted overview including emotional contrast, he was excited to talk about his guitar-playing and writing achievements. He cringed when he mentioned his role as a data analyst. He discovered that his experience as a child of divorce enhanced his ability to communicate.

He felt grounded in his Heart Value and recognized that, in the past, he had run away from unfulfilling jobs. Managing people and data actually made him cringe. Now he wanted to run toward experiences that related to his passions and brought him joy.

Sophie is a brilliant, savvy and creative executive in her fifties. When her company offered her an early retirement package, she took it because the company dynamics had changed and she no longer felt emotionally connected to the company's direction.

With the rise of technological advances and social media engagement, there is a perception that professionals in their forties, fifties and sixties don't offer the same value as younger folks. Many talented individuals are "let go" or "asked to retire" even when their institutional knowledge, firsthand experience and business savvy are beyond valuable.

Even though Sophie could financially afford to retire, her mind, body and soul craved a new purpose that would allow her Heart Value to shine. Sophie had tremendous value to offer and, above all else, she wanted to feel appreciated in her next endeavor.

Her Value Vault, a two-page timeline of pivotal moments and personal attributes, revealed that her proudest moments occurred when she bravely coached others to make informed career choices. It also revealed her regrets, like when she sacrificed her travel plans and interests to meet the company's business demands. She realized that, even in the most challenging of circumstances, one of her superpowers was helping others to use their talents.

Forty-two-year-old Danny is smart, competent and hardworking, but he lacked confidence. Throughout his tenure in one long-term position, he received exceptional performance reviews that clearly validated his contributions, but there was an emotional disconnect with his boss.

Danny was not "one of the boys" and always felt misunderstood at work. His manager didn't see Danny's Heart Value, so he used a reorganization to eliminate Danny's role when the company fell on some challenging financial times.

Of course, Danny internalized this layoff as his failure. His ego was bruised, and he felt embarrassed that, at his age, he needed to find a new job to support his family.

Danny's Value Vault was a colorful, categorized mind map. Through this exercise, he rediscovered his love for managing and presenting research to improve product life cycles. He proudly and consistently hit his True Stride when that was his primary responsibility.

He admitted that working for that particular boss made company politics cringeworthy, but if he could find a similar role with a boss who genuinely appreciated him, then he'd be thrilled. He also realized a pattern of happiness related to his health priorities. When he committed to working out regularly and imbibing less, everything else in life flowed more easily.

CREATIVE WAYS TO DISPLAY YOUR VALUE VAULT

What if you regularly gave yourself permission to appreciate the good, the bad and the ugly? Your expansion experiences—whether professional accomplishments, personal achievements, hurtful hiccups, entertaining encounters, comical crossroads or devastating detours—are your story to tell, in whatever creative format you choose to share.

You don't have to make it a deep dive, like I did. You can create a bulleted overview, like Rocky; a timeline, like Sophie; or a colorful mind map, like Danny. Do what feels right to you. The key is to deepen your understanding of your value and strategically use your feelings, choices and actions to align with your True Stride. Here are a few of my Value Vault examples to get you started.

Tangible Example	Value Gained	Emotional Contrast	Heart Value (Y/N)
Professional: Conducted sales enablement, systems, product, change management, and other trainings	Communications, speaking, training, teaching, empowering others	Proud and energized	Yes to speaking, teaching and training
Professional: Deployed complex products, systems and software	Teamwork, strategic planning	Proud I acquired those skills, but the work no longer lights me up; drained	No to large-scale initiatives
Personal: Completed two marathons; trained for two others	Dedication, planning, discipline, strength, self-love, saying "no" to people and things that interfered with training	Proud and energized	Yes to running; no to long distances

Personal: Moved over ten times; purchased one co-op and three homes; sold one co-op and two homes	Packing and moving skills, staging homes, negotiation; yes, I am Queen of Tetris when packing boxes and vehicles	Cringe; it was necessary but never fun	No; I loathe moving
Expansion: Cancer diagnosis	Became extremely health-conscious, empathetic, appreciative of life's little moments; gained unique perspective on life and meaningful relationships	Pride in managing my way; cringe over different challenges I faced	Yes to sharing if it helps others; no to focusing on it outside of doctors' visits
Expansion: Divorce and miscarriage	Empathy, health priorities, communication, connection, self-love, importance of teamwork and partnership; willing to share lessons if it helps others	Cringe; both were painful and draining	No

MARY TESS ROONEY

WHY IT MATTERS TO INVEST IN YOUR VALUE VAULT

For starters, appreciation starts with you! Taking inventory of your expansive Heart Value is extremely powerful and offers more fulfillment than any external award, accolade or promotion ever will. Seeing your value, with tangible examples, reinforces the fact that you already have and offer extreme value!

Wouldn't it be nice if your Value Vault was easily referenced and relatable? Your imprint, who you are and how you make an impact matter. You are constantly accruing value, so this is your living and breathing testament that, once drafted, can be easily updated, referenced and enhanced as you continue on your adventure.

Internally, taking time to see and feel your Heart Value increases your self-confidence as you use your past and present to strategically advise your future. Many amazing people struggle to share their value with pride; allow yourself to push past old limiting beliefs to honor your value.

Externally, your documented Value Vault will empower your ability to Activate Appreciation as you decide to increase your visibility, voice, confidence and more. Imagine a world where self-promotion, based on concrete examples, is celebrated—where every individual is proud to own, promote and celebrate their growth.

Rocky, Sophie and Danny each did an amazing job of investing in their Value Vault and listing all their experiences—yes, the good, the bad, the ugly and the complicated—as an accumulation of their value. Each approached the documentation process differently—a bulleted overview by theme, a timeline of pivotal moments and personal attributes, a colorful, categorized mind map—but that's the fun and creative part of expressing your value. They all illustrated their Heart Value, superpowers and Achilles' heels in unique ways that resonated for them.

And they all took time to analyze and hold each Value Vault gem to understand how that experience made them feel. The emotional contrast that surfaced provided clues as to how they might move toward their something. They knew what experiences they hoped to repeat, and they honed in on activities to definitely avoid.

The act of courageously telling your story leads to increased confidence, visibility, joy and appreciation. Rocky, Sophie and Danny were each now primed to use their past and present to strategically advise their future. That's the power of your Value Vault; you see your value and feel connected to what truly matters.

Reviewing your tangible examples, compelling stories and impactful results, in tandem with each emotional response, encourages you to follow your Heart Value. If you want to direct your path toward more experiences that light you up and bring you joy, investing in your Value Vault is the best gift you can give yourself.

CHECKPOINT: YOUR VALUE VAULT INVESTMENT

As you reflect, notice your emotional responses. Each heart-centered feeling provides clues that will influence your choices and inform your actions.

Instrumental Insights

- Don't wait for an invitation to voice your value. It's worth the investment!

- Your Value Vault holds your treasured successes, your impressive fails and everything in between, including how each experience makes you feel. Your Value Vault is a physical, mental and emotional account of all the experiences that make you, *you*.

- Personal satisfaction and public recognition can coexist. Don't minimize or discount your value.

MARY TESS ROONEY

- An expansion experience is a moment, interaction or milestone that increases your value. Acceptance allows you and others to benefit from that lesson.

- Invest in your Value Vault today and commit to an ongoing practice. The act of telling your story leads to increased confidence, visibility and appreciation.

- Evaluate the emotional contrast that surfaces with each Value Vault acknowledgment. Remember to pay attention to what makes you proud or cringe as you move forward.

WISE WALK REFLECTION

Journal without judgment and process these Wise Walk questions to gain awareness.

1. As you recall a Value Vault experience—personal, professional or expansion—ask yourself: How does that gem entry make you feel? What emotional contrast surfaces for you? Does the experience make you feel proud or make you cringe, make you feel energized or drained, make you feel joy and satisfaction or a sense of deflation?

2. Knowing your feelings connected to each experience is powerful. What *choices* will you make to experience more joy, satisfaction, energy and pride as you share your value with this world?

3. Are you ready to unlock your Value Vault and create an actionable plan to attract more appreciation and joy?

FEEL-CHOOSE-ACT AMPLIFIER

Observe an area in your life that you'd like to address and apply this feel, choose and act amplifier. Jump right in, or read the example below to get your Feel-Choose-Act juices flowing.

Feel	Choose	Act

Feel	Choose	Act
I felt frustrated that I needed to document my value in a different way to be seen, but I was also motivated and inspired to appreciate my treasured successes, impressive fails and everything in between in a new way.	I made a choice to invest in my Value Vault, which surfaced my expansive value and how each experience made me feel. I began to make choices that allowed me to receive personal satisfaction and public recognition.	The emotional contrast was eye-opening, so I began to selectively release actions that didn't light me up anymore and voice my value for the contributions I wanted to share more.

MARY TESS ROONEY

Affirmation

I treasure all my value and the experiences that have made me, me. I proudly voice my value to receive the appreciation, recognition and satisfaction I deserve.

Tip:

This act of acknowledging the emotional contrast for each Value Vault entry allows you to use your past and present to strategically advise your future. Don't get overwhelmed. Start small and respect your feelings, whatever they are.

Notes:

Get Your Stride On

You are constantly gaining value. With age, your expansion experiences and value stack up. Don't forget to be like Paul Revere and write a first-person account of all of it!

Endnotes

4   Survivor, *CBS*, 2000-2020, https://www.cbs.com/shows/survivor/.

CHAPTER 5

READ THE SIGNS: TRUST YOUR INNER COMPASS

We felt stuck—trapped by our own mental chains, made-up rules and limiting beliefs.

Eva, a technology executive in her forties, had a consistent track record of working for start-ups, building exceptional customer relations teams, increasing profits and then reaping the financial rewards post-IPO. By all accounts, she was a leader in high demand, and she loved offering her value.

Eva was confident in her talents and abilities. She was a high achiever who prided herself on fostering success for herself and others. She consistently turned the most disgruntled customers into loyal lifelong clients. She delivered results, and the board, employees and shareholders all raved about her impact.

Despite her success, Eva admitted on the phone one evening that she was unhappy at work. Her boss, Silas, the president of the company, did not appreciate her and was constantly challenging her ideas and recommendations. Because she loved the team she had built and valued her impeccable track record, Eva was determined to win Silas over.

Silas spoke to her with disdain or questioned her direction without cause. At first, this energetic disconnect caused Eva sleepless nights. Then an ulcer. As time went on, she began to break out in hives before she had to meet with him.

Sadly, Eva never found her True Stride while working for Silas. After fourteen months of strategizing ways to improve their toxic relationship, remaining strong for her team, providing exceptional customer service and sacrificing valuable personal and family fulfillment, she finally raised the white flag. Had her body's physical, mental and emotional signs not screamed at her to leave the hostile work environment, she may have continued to press on.

Eva didn't do anything to provoke Silas's disapproval, but she had programmed herself to persevere and work the problem until it was fixed. As she looks back, her biggest regret is that she read the signs within the first few weeks on the job, and yet it took her over a year to make a change.

To *read the signs* means to receive, accept and interpret a physical, mental, emotional or spiritual message that steers us toward our highest good. Signs can appear in all forms. People, places, activities and things that come into our lives have the potential to expand our thinking, inspire new interests, raise red flags or completely redirect our course.

For individuals like Eva, me and perhaps you, the ability to read the signs can be difficult when we're too attached to our original plan and desired outcome. The attachment to our commitment and expectations overpowers our ability to openly receive and read the signs.

Eva's nurturing, never-let-anyone-down side led her to suppress her feelings for

MARY TESS ROONEY

the sake of her team and the company. Her principled sense of obligation mandated that she *should* give it at least a year. That conventional thinking was her own made-up rule.

Although Eva definitely learned a ton from that experience and made the best of her predicament, it came at an extremely high opportunity cost. Instead of focusing her value, time and energy on her health, happiness, loved ones and overall well-being, she wasted her precious value, time and energy on people who didn't appreciate her Heart Value.

Eva and I are cut from the same cloth. Unfortunately, I too have been guilty of ignoring, rationalizing or resisting signs because of my sense of responsibility, commitment or attachment. I've persisted too long on a chosen path at the expense of my health. Or I stayed in an unhealthy relationship because I was attached to a dream instead of reality.

I'm not encouraging you to abandon your path at the first sign of resistance, only to pay attention and be open to information that enters your life. Your capacity to read the signs, without judgment, can improve your current path, show you additional possibilities or nudge you in a new direction.

While I was attending Boston College, a roommate of one of my varsity crew teammates, Faith, got pregnant. I remember sitting in the dining hall when she told me her news. I promptly replied, "Congratulations! That's exciting. How far along are you?"

Faith burst into hysterical tears. At first, I was taken aback, thinking, "Oh, no, I said something wrong!" I sincerely apologized

> **To read the signs** means to receive, accept and interpret a message that steers you toward your highest good.

Notes:

to Faith for inadvertently upsetting her. I was friends with her roommate but didn't know Faith, so I had zero context before I spoke. My words flowed out before I had time to think about them.

Faith quickly reassured me that they were tears of joy. I had been the first person, out of all her friends and family, who gave her a positive response versus seeing this unplanned pregnancy as a tragic mistake. She was barraged with well-meaning advice about giving the baby up for adoption, but not one person in her immediate family thought she was ready to be a mom. She didn't blame her loved ones for pointing out the complications she would face as a single parent given her young age, her non-relationship with the father, her lack of financial means and the disruption in her college education. However, our brief exchange illuminated her desire to raise this baby despite the impending hardships.

Feel
Choose
Act
Trust Your Inner Compass

Faith had been praying for clarity and courage to follow the right path for her. She admitted—to herself and the entire breakfast table—that she felt like this pregnancy was a blessing.

MARY TESS ROONEY

One supportive comment helped Faith read her signs and emotionally connect to what felt right for her. It wasn't logical or practical, but she realigned with her Heart Value and discovered a moment of relief.

The more you pay attention to signs and trust your inner compass, the more you'll strengthen your ability to realize your True Stride. You know what's best for you. The number one person you should honor and trust is yourself. That's not selfish—that's self-love.

Are you ready to receive messages, process options and observe your reality without attachment? What choices have you made that are not aligned with your True Stride? Do you currently take time to read the signs and reflect on how your current situation makes you feel? What flags are surfacing in your life, and what do they mean in terms of the direction you are headed?

FREEDOM TO CHOOSE AGAIN

When I pursued my coaching certificate, the phrase "freedom to choose again" surfaced during one of our triad coaching sessions. Tim was the coach, Rose was the client and I was the observer.

Rose, a mother in her late thirties, felt stuck, unhappy and judgmental of her present mindset. She admitted that before she married, she told her husband that she wanted to be a stay-at-home mom and raise their kids. Fast-forward five years and two kids later, and they were living the life they'd planned together. She loved her kids and her hubby, but she was absolutely glum in the role of full-time mother and household caregiver.

As Tim probed deeper, Rose made comments like, "I agreed to play this role. I *should* continue until the kids are out of school." "I *ought to* enjoy it more—it's what I always said I wanted." "It wouldn't be fair to my husband or my kids to go back to work; *they deserve* to have the life we envisioned for them."

When Tim asked Rose what she wanted for herself, she responded, "Well, I *should…*" Immersed in her own world of *shoulds* and *ought tos*, she couldn't see a scenario where she was allowed to experience joy for herself.

The first time I realized Rose was living her life according to everyone else's ideals—even the ones she cherished before she became a mom—I got chills down my spine. It was one of those aha moments that I will never forget.

Perhaps her struggle forced me to take a hard look at my own life. From the outside, it seemed ideal. A respectable corporate job with benefits. A house in the suburbs. Loving and supportive friends and family. I *ought to* be happy. There was my own ought…ugh.

This realization was a wake-up call for me and this obliging stay-at-home mom. We both felt stuck and trapped by our own mental chains, made-up rules and limiting beliefs. We thought doing the right thing meant staying on our respective paths, which no longer brought us joy even though we once chose them. We were focused on what seemed right for *others*, at the expense of our own fulfillment.

In some way, we viewed our inexperienced choices as life or long-term sentences. Are you, in any way, living a punitive sentence of your own making?

Eva gave herself a one-year sentence for making a bad career choice. She had the power to change her situation at any moment. She wasn't under contract, but she didn't give herself permission to change her mind and choose again despite all the signs.

Rose imposed a motherhood sentence on herself before she knew what that experience entailed. Once she faced the fact that her commitment made her miserable, she created space to unpack her feelings and prioritize her dreams. With Tim, she acknowledged that *she deserved* to feel happy, too. She planned to honestly discuss her feelings with her husband as a first step.

I had convinced myself that I *should* want what others deemed desirable and good for me. I didn't want to disappoint anyone. I had responsibilities, financial obligations and employees who were counting on me. I couldn't let them down. I'm not a quitter.

And then, like a lightning bolt piercing right through my core, a simple and powerful question struck me and kept repeating in my head. What if I gave myself the freedom to choose again?

What if I released all my shoulds and ought tos, and looked deep inside my soul to discover what truly brings me joy? What would my life's path and happiness look like then?

I have no idea what Rose ended up choosing for herself. I only know that her honesty and courage inspired me to evaluate my own path and armed me with self-permission instead of a self-imposed life sentence. The mantra *freedom to choose again* became my grounding phrase as I began to read the signs and intentionally invite more joy into my life.

When was the last time you gave yourself permission to choose again, if the reality of your plan created misery and hurt your health, energy and most cherished relationships?

There have been several times in my life when I got locked into this idea of completing the task before me because I was a rule follower or I didn't want to disappoint others. I lacked balance. I was so externally driven by responsibility and approval that I allowed my personal life, overall well-being and joy to suffer. Back then, I didn't have a process to gut-check myself so—no joke—there were assignments that landed me in the hospital. But recalling the emotional contrast of joy and suffering empowered me to create a gut-check practice that now keeps me connected to my True Stride.

Like Eva and Rose, I had clarity and awareness around what was and was not working in my life. This wake-up call motivated me to trust my inner compass and begin to envision a different adventure for myself.

The signs were clear, but at that juncture, I was solely responsible for two mortgages in two areas with extremely high property taxes. While I was ready to give myself permission to choose again, extracting myself from things that did not bring me joy or no longer served me would take time. Thankfully, I knew that if I started to take steps, however small, the momentum would shift over time and I'd hit my True Stride.

It felt like I had been lost in the forest, and this decision allowed me to cut through the brush to chart a new path. The biggest challenge for me is usually getting going. I wasn't exactly sure where I was going or how long it would take, but my something was calling and I knew how I wanted to *feel*. My heart-centered inner compass was calling me to envision a destination where I felt energized and happy in all that I do.

All of us possess an internal knowing of what is right for us, but sometimes we get distracted by external pressures or expectations and forget how to trust it. Or we lose our way, struggle to listen to our hearts and don't take the time to ground ourselves to get back on the track that feels right for us.

For most of my life, I relied on my ability to observe, self-reflect and take thoughtful action—but at some junctures, I forgot to lead with my heart.

Our hearts are at the center of our inner compass, and the key to navigating this adventure we call life. When we learn to listen to and lead from our heart, our inner compass becomes more accurate and better equipped to direct us.

Think about this: Our hearts are vital to sustain life. Our hearts are central to everything we do, but sometimes we put our focus elsewhere.

Our minds are important too, but it's not the mind that informs our emotions or affects our energy, directly impacting our experiences. It's the heart.

And isn't it interesting that we can survive without brain waves and activity, but we can't live without our heart. Our unique heartbeat. Our pulse.

Your heart is unique to you; so is every person's. No one has your heartbeat. The

MARY TESS ROONEY

heart's size, shape, valves, age, structure, fitness level and more all create a unique rhythm, pulse and beat.

If you experience life from your brain, you're missing the vital experience from your heart. Your heart is a muscle that fuels every other organ and requires physical and emotional exercise to be in top condition. And good or bad, you feel it in your heart first. When you honor your heart's response, you have a full experience. Your brain can play a role, but we'd all benefit if we followed our hearts' feedback first. Your brain is exceptional at remembering your successful patterns and repetition, but your heart is the central mechanism that directs your inner compass.

This idea is so important to me that I even made up a phrase, Heart Vibe, to help me honor this sentiment and lead with my heart's feedback. For me, Heart Vibe means feeling the frequency within your heart and using that information to guide your inner compass.

Since every interaction and situation makes you feel or vibrate an energy, you have the ability to pay attention to what makes your heart feel happy, or dims your vibration and makes it feel heavy. Your Heart Vibe sparks or drops based on what you feel in each experience.

What I've learned, from my own experiences and in working with others, is that what you *feel*—in your heart—is so powerful. The key to any meaningful discovery is to seek and attract what

Heart Vibe is your ability to sense how experiences and external elements (people, places, activities and things) awaken your heart or dim your light.

Notes:

really matters to your Heart Vibe so that you can feel, choose and act with intention.

Whether you are spiritual or not, we all experience moments on our path when signs appear. Sometimes the signs are subtle messages that ring through our souls, as I experienced in my observer role during Rose's coaching session. Rose never knew how her paralyzed rationale of shoulds and ought tos helped me see my life differently. I had to be attuned to my inner compass to understand its significance in my life.

At other times, the signs are blatant—they give you hives or trigger a massive emotional release as you try to wash away unnerving events. Either way, when you take time and space to read the signs, you receive clarity, support or a needed nudge to intentionally move forward. These signs will reinforce your current path or provide insight to consider a new direction.

It's your responsibility to receive, accept and interpret these messages to move closer to your highest good. Loving and caring for yourself is good for you and everyone around you.

Be alert and open to reshaping your path if and when you feel unaligned. If something feels off, you have the *freedom to choose again*. Don't penalize yourself for inexperience by creating a self-imposed misery sentence. It doesn't serve you or those around you.

When "flags" surface, trust your inner compass and use your feelings to inform your path forward. With your fresh understanding of what resonates and doesn't, your chosen direction will help you get from a starting point to a specific destination.

I pay attention not just to red flags, but green, yellow and white flags too.

Red flags are metaphorical signals that something is wrong. A red flag in your life could indicate an obstacle or an emotional trigger in your path that causes a momentary reflection, stop or redirection. Overall, they signal you to pay attention before you proceed. Sometimes red flags are intuitive warnings that say a certain path is not aligned with your Heart Value. Sometimes they are old patterns we have to break, such as a limiting belief or a dynamic with an unsupportive family member, before we can move forward.

Green flags are historically used to indicate that all systems are go. As with traffic lights, they signal it's safe to move forward because you have the right of way. A green flag in your life reinforces that you are headed in the right direction. Enjoy your progress as your path brings you one step closer to achieving your goal.

Yellow flags represent the need to proceed with caution. Yellow flags make us slow down, pause or prepare to stop.

White flags mean surrender for something better. Often, when you hold onto something that is not working in your life, letting go can help make room for what will work. When a white flag appears, ask yourself what you need to release in order to move forward.

Your inner compass provides directional insights based on your energetic, emotional, physical, mental and spiritual awareness. When you are attuned to your inner compass, you are in harmony and moving in alignment with your Heart Value. This gut check process empowers you to navigate your flags and paths to live your best adventure.

Read The Signs

Trust Your Inner Compass

Freedom to Choose

CHECKPOINT: TRUST YOUR *INNER* COMPASS

As you reflect, notice your emotional responses. Each heart-centered feeling that surfaces provides clues that will influence your choices and inform your actions.

Instrumental Insights

- ~ "Read the signs" is about using your feelings to become aware of what *is* and *is not* working well in your life.

- ~ Release your sense of responsibility or attachment that causes you to ignore, rationalize or resist flags and signs.

- ~ Channel how you want to feel as a destination and gut-check your progress to inform your path, reclaim your power and align with your Heart Value.

- ~ People, places, activities and things deliver signs. It's your responsibility to receive, accept and interpret those messages to make choices and take action toward your highest good.

- ~ Be alert and open to reshaping your path if and when you *feel* unaligned. Don't view inexperienced choices as a life or long-term misery sentence. Freedom to choose again gives you permission to redirect your path at any time.

WISE WALK REFLECTION

Journal without judgment and let your thoughts, feelings, choices and actions flow as a stream of consciousness.

1. What area of your life *feels unaligned*? What types of signs are appearing in your life? Physical signs: in your environment or body, like traffic jams or sickness. Advice signs: someone unexpectedly sharing eye-opening information. Metaphysical signs: interesting coincidences. How will you use those feelings to guide your inner compass? Are you taking time to read those signs?

2. Have you ever penalized yourself for inexperience and created a self-imposed short- or long-term sentence, like Eva? What choice would you make differently, if you could? If you give yourself the freedom to choose again, what new decision will bring you closer to where you want to go?

3. After you receive, accept and interpret signs from people, places and things, what's one thing you will start doing today to *act* on them?

FEEL-CHOOSE-ACT AMPLIFIER

Observe an area in your life that you'd like to address and apply this feel, choose and act amplifier. Jump right in, or read the following examples to get your Feel-Choose-Act juices flowing.

Feel	Choose	Act

Feel > Choose > Act

Feel	Choose	Act
When I experience physical and emotional signs that I'm not on the right path, I pay attention. I use my feelings to understand what is and is not aligned with my Heart Value.	I give myself the freedom to choose again if my inexperience led me down one path, only for me to realize that something feels off. I don't need to analyze or justify what feels off. What's important is to give myself permission to choose again, to make a different choice for myself.	Once I'm clear on what choices are available to me, I trust my inner compass and take action.
Eva felt an energetic and emotional disconnect from her boss, and her body manifested signs of sleepless nights, an ulcer and hives for her to read.	She knew she was unhappy, but she made a choice to stay for a year because she was determined to succeed, protect her team and win him over.	Finally, Eva couldn't overlook her body's physical and emotional signs—so she resigned. Her biggest regret is that she wishes she would have acted sooner, because she's very happy and appreciated in a new job now.

Affirmation

I am alert and proficient at reading the signs, which expands my thinking, inspires new interests and redirects my course.

Muscle memory is a skill and ability that becomes our own unconscious response. It's a movement or pattern that becomes second nature after consistent practice, like brushing your teeth or driving a car.

Tip:

Your ability to read the signs and apply what you've learned gets easier over time. The key is to listen to your inner compass as you move forward, which creates muscle memory. The more you trust your inner compass and exercise this feel-choose-act mantra, the more natural it becomes. Eventually it becomes second nature.

Notes:

Notes:

Get Your Stride On

What if you gave yourself the "freedom
to choose again"?

CHAPTER 6

PRIORITIZE FUN: ELEVATE YOUR JOY FREQUENCY

*I had forgotten that it is acceptable, even admirable, to prioritize
things that mattered to me first and foremost.*

For years, the print, editorial and online publication *Outside*, which inspires "active participation in the world outside," has published an annual article on the "Best Places to Work" based on companies that prioritize work-life balance in welcoming environments.

I love *Outside*'s mission, pursuit of outdoor inspiration and encouragement of their readers to "take [their] wonder outside," but the term "work-life balance" makes me cringe. The aim of "work-life balance" is to reduce stress and prevent burnout but, to be candid, I never attained that elusive goal in any of my Fortune 100 careers.

The Muse, a New York-based, content-rich recruitment site connecting more than 75 million job seekers with research, career paths, professional advancement, skill-building and coaching, highlights leading companies on their website that "actively cultivate a sense of joy and fun at work." Although the companies pay to be featured on their website under "The 30 Greatest Companies to Work for This Year (That are All Hiring Right Now!)"[5], the Muse disclaims that since those companies are aligned with the Muse's values, they are happy to feature them and it's not a conflict of interest. Their post states, "Take Appian, whose Virginia campus (only fifteen miles outside of Washington, D.C.) has a one-mile running path and an on-site gym. Or Shutterstock, whose New York office boasts game rooms and open mic nights."

I enjoyed reading about the Muse's "30 Greatest Companies" and *Outside*'s "50 Best Places to Work"[6] (I read the 2019 article), and all eighty companies seem super cool. Sadly, out of the fifty best places to work featured in *Outside*, I had only heard of three of them. That's not an overwhelming endorsement for companies standing behind work-life balance as a "priority."

In my own experience, incorporating more balance in offices and cultures was often spoken about and superficially encouraged, followed by, "Oh and how soon can you have that report on my desk?"

I don't know about you, but I always wanted to reduce stress and infuse "a sense of joy and fun" into my work. As I went back over *Outside*'s list of fifty to calculate how many employees were benefiting from the featured employers' pioneering work-life efforts, the grand total rang in at 3,209. Ugh. For a national publication with 3.4 million active readers, that's a very small statistical pool to play in.

In 2019, the employed population of the United States included approximately 156 million people. The largest company on *Outside*'s 2019 list had 773 employees. There were several boutiques on that list that had only 15 employees.

I couldn't help but wonder how other *Outside* readers felt as they absorbed this article.

MARY TESS ROONEY

Did they feel encouraged by the focus, dedication and out-of-the-box thinking of these admirable fifty? Or did they feel deflated, as I did, knowing that while those fifty companies certainly deserve recognition and praise, we need more to follow their lead? What's it going to take to impact more than 3,209 employees in a workforce of approximately 156 million Americans?

WHAT DOES PRIORITIZE FUN MEAN?

The biggest challenge I see with the abstract work-life commentary is that it relies on companies to offer better work-life solutions to bolster employee satisfaction. In Chapter 4, you reclaimed your power—so why give it away? *Let go* of that unicorn pursuit of a company that will give you balance. You can decide to *prioritize fun* on your own terms. The result will be more joy in your life, daily!

After everything you've learned, applied and embraced from the previous chapters, you are in a prime position to maximize your energetic vibration, feel appreciated in ways that matter and realize your True Stride. You have successfully invested in your Value Vault. You trust your inner compass and use your value and appreciation sweet spot to advise your future. Woo-hoo!!

You have strengthened your Heart Value muscles, and the momentum of your True Stride will continue to groove as you apply those skills. In this chapter, I invite you to commit to prioritizing fun as you apply all you've learned so far.

I love the *prioritize fun* oxymoron!

The word *prioritize* is usually a work or business term, which

> To **prioritize fun** means to reserve, block and protect time in your day to experience joy and awaken your Heart Vibe.

Notes:

means to designate or treat something as more important than other things, while the word *fun* has a childlike, joyful appeal and means amusement and lighthearted pleasure.

This contrasting combination of labor and gratification is exactly what's necessary to establish more balance and harmony in your life. And not just during your "office hours," but in all aspects of your life.

I've surveyed hundreds of people and asked them, "In your daily list of to-dos, do you prioritize fun?"

Ninety percent laughed heartily at that question, as if I was pulling their leg or asking them something completely ridiculous.

When they realized I was asking sincerely—thanks to my NYC, raised-eyebrow "for reals" stare—most participants in my non-qualitative, unscientific survey expressed that they viewed *fun* as an afterthought or didn't see *fun* as important when considering their daily objectives.

Their general sentiment was, "*If* I get all of my to-dos done, then I incorporate fun." Or, "My days are so overscheduled that I can only afford to have fun on the weekends, and again, that's *if* I get all my chores done." Or, "Isn't that what vacation is for?"

There's a societal belief that responsibilities, work, obligations and commitments should all come before the so-called guilty pleasures of fun. You must get all your work done before you can relax, enjoy a favorite pastime or do something silly to replenish your energy.

In general, the end-of-day question is, "What did you *do* today?" Not, "In what ways did you have *fun* today?" Or, "How did you *prioritize fun* today?"

We've decided that if fun doesn't have a meaningful purpose, then it's unnecessary for existence. We've deemed fun a reward, to be enjoyed once hard work and results are proven, but isn't that another made-up rule?

Somewhere along the line, we designated fun as frivolous. We were taught to admire hard work and delayed gratification. No one gets points for surfing, taking a nature walk or watching TV in the middle of the day. Instead, people who do those things are perceived as slackers or flippant about their professions.

The number one response when I ask the question, "What prevents you from experiencing fun during your day?" is, "There's not enough time in the day." In reality, the great equalizer in life is that we all have exactly the same number of hours in each day. The difference is in how we choose to spend those hours.

One of my favorite executives, Collin, is a runner. When he learned I was a runner too, he suggested that the next time we have business items to discuss, we do so over a six-mile run. I loved this idea because I could log my miles for the day while getting his guidance on the multiple projects I was managing.

We had some of our most productive and solution-oriented meetings on our runs. Collin had the ability to run an eight-minute mile, but we kept our runs to a conversational, ten-minute-mile pace to tackle our pressing work objectives.

It was productive and fun to discuss our projects on New York City's Central Park running paths. Collin was grateful that we shared the same passion for exercise and running, and he was pleased that I was open to scheduling our meetings so we could kill two birds with one stone—work and play. It was freeing to ditch the suit and the boardroom for trees, nature and the presence of other outdoor enthusiasts.

Collin and I literally prioritized fun and got our work done. This strategy of combining work and enjoyment can apply to so many other areas of your life, as long as you open your mind to the possibilities.

You don't necessarily need a company's stamp of approval to prioritize fun or infuse balance into your life. Take the time to brainstorm ways to prioritize fun in your daily activities so it doesn't become an afterthought.

How are you prioritizing your time?

WHAT WILL BE REMEMBERED

My friend Quinn was in shock when she called to tell me about the passing of her dear friend, Tristan, a forty-eight-year-old realtor. As she shared Tristan's tragic timeline, there was one random detail that I couldn't shake for days.

The night before Tristan's unexpected death, he made an elaborate Southern-style caramel cake that took him over three hours to make from scratch, bake and decorate. For him, this was a creation of passion and love.

I didn't know Tristan, so I couldn't help but wonder: If he knew he had one day to live, would he have invested so much time in his cake creation? The phrase "what will be remembered when we are gone" lingered in my mind, followed by, "At least he prioritized fun, in a way that mattered to him, before he passed on."

Unexpected deaths are the toughest to accept and process because you question what you said or didn't say, did or didn't do prior to your loss. It's also unnerving because it makes you reflect and take inventory of how you spend your time each day.

If you knew that today was your last day on earth, what would you prioritize? Are you grounded in what a successful day *feels* like to you? How often do you feel joyful at the end of your day?

ADDICTED TO DOING VERSUS BEING

I remember Hazel telling me that her industry change, from managing communications in a media company to a pharmaceutical company, was agonizing because the businesses' priorities were extremely different. For a communications professional, the paces in these settings are polar opposites. In media, leaders want everything done yesterday and then reactively change their minds, so she was constantly on. In the pharmaceutical industry, leaders hypothesize about communications needs for products that *may* be available in ten years, so there's a thoughtful and methodical planning process and the last-minute changes are negligible.

To her surprise, Hazel had become a communications adrenaline junkie who thrived on media's frantic, chaotic environment and was addicted to the relentless commotion. She didn't feel valuable if she wasn't constantly producing, editing and reacting to requests at warp speed. Her pharma company reassured her that she was exceeding their expectations, but Hazel's ego missed the rush of *feeling needed* and *doing*, from one metaphorical "fix" to the next.

As I listened to Hazel's story, I recognized that I could relate. Without knowing it, I had become a *doing* adrenaline junkie too and often prioritized the company's agenda ahead of my own personal priorities. My old belief system commended *doing* and applauded me for managing one crisis after the next with style, competence and grace.

"Lucky" for me, one year, my body literally revolted from my internal conflict between *do* and *be*. It took three hospital visits, surgery and a slow recovery to accept that the *doer* in me needed a time-out or, more accurately, to be benched.

Technically, I didn't produce anything tangible that year. But I had two major epiphanies that redefined my understanding of doing, being and daily priorities. My health crisis forced me to cancel multiple meetings and postpone the launch of my own business. On days I tried to keep the pace, participate in planned meetings and tend to action items, the negative ramifications for my health were debilitating.

If I thought I was feeling better or that I could muscle through, bam! I'd regress. I became keenly aware that I was physically unable to overschedule and prioritize others' needs above my own, especially if I wanted to fully recover.

When I actually established healthy boundaries and put this insight into practice, the reality was that no one was phased or even impacted. People adapted once I communicated my shift in priorities. The world kept spinning and everyone lived their life as usual.

I realized that the pressure and expectations I felt were all self-created. There was no choice but to prioritize my medical needs and care. I had to become the chief executive officer of my biggest investment—me. Let's face it, without our health, nothing else really matters.

My Heart Value relationships stayed strong because the energetic and emotional connection I shared with these people meant they were invested in my overall well-being. People who genuinely cared about me were unconcerned with what I *did* during the day. They cared about who I was as a human, friend and loved one. Heart Value relationships are in it for the long haul, so a year or more over the span of decades is a blip.

I had forgotten that it is acceptable, even admirable, to prioritize things that mattered to me first and foremost. For that year and the months that followed, I was forced to prioritize my health and healing. I was harshly reminded that life is too precious and fragile not to make my health a priority.

The much-needed break from all the hustle and bustle I had previously invited into my life empowered me to reconsider how I chose to spend my precious time. It's amazing how being forced to stop filling your days and clear your calendar fosters deep insight into what deserves to reclaim a spot.

CALENDAR TIDYING UP

If you've ever watched the Netflix's series *Tidying Up*[7] with Marie Kondo, the well-known author who guides people to declutter their homes using a category-by-category focus, you know that she requires each participant to take all of their clothing items and place them on the bed. The completely empty closet represents a blank canvas, and participants are empowered to carefully select and rehang only the items that align with their real selves.

MARY TESS ROONEY

As in Kondo's book, aspiring declutterers are instructed to hold each piece of clothing and determine whether it brings them joy. If the article "sparks joy," they can proudly hang it back up in the closet. If it does not, they thank the item for its service and place it in a rehome, donate or discard pile.

Any minimalist expert will say that the benefit of seeing your carefully selected clothing items sparsely and neatly displayed in your closet is that you are constantly reminded of what brings you joy. Your clothing priorities (so to speak) are in plain sight, out in the open, and serve as daily reminders of the ease and focus with which you have chosen to apply joy to your day.

Since I didn't *do* or produce much of anything that year, I had the opportunity to use this approach with my calendar. The empty closet was similar to my barren calendar. I questioned each activity to determine if it supported my True Stride and aligned with who I wanted to be.

With a laser focus on inviting more of a *being* mentality, I thoughtfully considered what daily activities brought me joy. I asked myself, what *doing* items did I want to liberate, delegate or abandon?

As I applied this minimalist practice to my calendar, nine themes surfaced:

~ Root	~ Purpose	~ Contribute
~ Meditate	~ Reflect	~ Manifest
~ Exercise	~ Nourish	~ Express

When I reviewed the nine, they naturally fell into three overarching categories: fuel my body, awaken my heart and energize my soul.

Through the process of trial and experience, I've discovered that my joy frequency is highest when my daily actions incorporate the nine themes (root, purpose, contribute, meditate, reflect, manifest, exercise, nourish and express). When I neglect one or multiple areas in my life on any given day, my joy frequency suffers. Similarly, I've learned the hard way that fueling my body, awakening my heart and energizing my soul works best for my overall well-being. Below are a few examples of activities that I try to engage in every day to raise my joy frequency. I call it the Joy Frequency Grid because these choices and actions supply me with joyful energy. And yes, it is possible to integrate fun in all categories, so remember to prioritize fun as the forefront of your actions, not an afterthought.

> The **Joy Frequency Grid** is a visual tool created to remind you of your daily habits and actions that raise your energetic vibration and joy. Note: Mine has nine themes that roll into three overarching categories, but you can design your grid to support your unique well-being needs.

JOY FREQUENCY GRID

Energize Soul	**Purpose**	**Contribute**	**Root** (in Nature)
	Clarity on my legacy and which choices align or don't; ground in possible opportunities to contribute in a way that energizes my soul	Share my Heart Value, offer support, make a difference and be considerate in the lives of others; build supportive relationships	Ground in and appreciate nature's beauty and surroundings; enjoy sunrise and sunset, the garden, etc.

MARY TESS ROONEY

Awaken Heart	**Meditate**	**Reflect**	**Manifest**
	10-20 minutes of silent or guided time to be present and restore	Journal, read thought-provoking books or articles, listen to podcasts or music; create and review vision board	(Release & Set Intention) Liberate any negative thoughts, ideas, beliefs, people, activities, things, environments and fears that undermine my well-being; set intentions and use affirmations to evoke positivity and my something
Fuel Body	**Exercise**	**Nourish**	**Express**
	Run, practice yoga, walk, ski, snowboard, hike, bike, paddleboard, swim, golf, horseback ride, breathwork, Pilates	Probiotics, hydration, clean eating, nutrient-rich foods, easy digestion, fasting	Pay attention to inner compass and emotional contrast; allow my heart, mind and body's intuitive nature to speak up and use my voice to shine

Prioritize FUN across all checkpoints!!

Please note that *prioritize fun* is the thread within all categories. I consider each activity and then try to accomplish it in a spirit of fun. For example, meditation for ten to twenty minutes supercharges my day. I make choices about where and how I complete that practice. To prioritize fun while I meditate, I walk down to the beach at sunrise,

Joy Frequency refers to the level at which your vibration radiates harmony and blissful energy, inward and outward. Your goal is to have a high amount and occurrence of joy felt in your life, which means you consistently do things that light you up.

Notes:

watch the sun come up and then begin to meditate as the sound of my breath and ocean waves wash over me.

At the end of the day, how do you want your time to be used? Is your time jam-packed and overscheduled, or carefully planned to allow for fun to be part of each activity?

WHAT IS JOY FREQUENCY?

Joy Frequency is the level at which your vibration radiates harmony and blissful energy, inward and outward. Each time you trust your inner compass, honor your heart-centered value and feel appreciated in ways that matter, your joy frequency soars. When you don't authentically respect and prioritize one or more of those elements, you may struggle to align and fully experience joy.

MARY TESS ROONEY

Your heart constantly communicates clues to your bliss, if you listen. Being true to yourself and surrounding yourself with people who elevate your joy frequency makes all the difference in the world. We have to release this notion that we want everyone to love and appreciate us. In reality, we want to find our people, the tribe that matches our frequency and aligns with the value we offer.

As you strengthen your fluid movement to see value, feel appreciated and be your true self, your joy frequency naturally rises. This vibration radiates and encourages others to bravely lead with their heart to discover their True Stride too.

THE TEACHER IN ME

As a child, I had a lust for learning and a passion for teaching others. My younger sister, JJ, bore the brunt of my quest for knowledge and lesson-sharing. I have vivid memories of rushing home from school, sitting her in front of my chalkboard in the basement and reviewing whatever I had learned in class that day.

JJ, who is three years younger than me, ate it up and excelled. She was extremely smart and even started school a year early because she was so gifted. I loved her undivided attention, and seeing if I knew the content well enough to teach it.

My early obsession with teaching shot off from there. I learned intuitively how to prioritize fun while doing things I loved. I was an avid skier. I decided that teaching others to ski would give me more time on the slopes, a li'l cash and the fulfillment of teaching. I became a snowboard instructor and then a yoga instructor, got certified to teach consultative sales skills and change management, you name it.

The teacher in me is thrilled that you are reading this book. Thank you. I enjoy sharing what I've learned. And I'm excited for you to step fully into your True Stride and form meaningful Heart Value relationships that leave you feeling appreciated in ways that matter most.

TAP INTO YOUR CHILD PRIORITIES

Kids exemplify joytime. They find pleasure in the small things and laugh at almost anything. They give themselves permission to be silly. To prioritize play over chores. To discover what makes them happy and let their heart sing, over and over again.

I adore watching my nieces and nephews play a game, run with their whole bodies and try new activities with complete and utter freedom. Whether they are engaged in play, a video game, a magic trick, a TV program, a sport, a dance or whatever interests them, they fully commit.

In their playful zone, distractions are foreign to them. They are blessed with a singular focus. Their expectation is to have fun, so outside pressures do not penetrate their radar.

They also allow themselves to explore, be curious and choose again if the activity they started falls short of *their* expectations. Isn't it interesting that we encourage our kids to playfully honor what makes them happiest, but accept the notion that "adulting" means we don't get to play or make joytime a priority?

EXAMPLES OF WHAT BRINGS ME JOY

Joytime is a scheduled date or commitment to yourself to do something that brings you joy. In *The Artist's Way*[8], Julia Cameron encourages artists to schedule weekly creativity dates with themselves. She states, "An artist date is a block of time, perhaps two hours weekly, especially set aside and committed to nurturing your creative consciousness, your inner artist. In its most primary form, the artist date is an excursion, a play date that you preplan and defend against all interlopers."

You need alone time to connect with and inspire your creativity. To foster more joy in your life, you need to prioritize fun on a daily basis and block out joytime to nurture your inner child.

When I think about my moments of deep satisfaction and joy, I'm happiest outdoors among family, friends and other adventurous spirits who support my quest for laughter and exploration. Daily physical activity and reconnection with my body bring me joy. And yet, before I left the corporate world, I made "the job" more important than "the joy." I rarely took a day off just for myself.

If you took a day off, what would you do? What is the best way you experience joy?

Joytime is a scheduled date or commitment to yourself to do something that brings you joy.

Notes:

Jenn's ideal vacation is sitting on the beach with cocktails and a good book. She loves to read, and the act of giving herself permission to immerse herself in an author's reality brings her great satisfaction.

Mike loves becoming a mountain man to recharge. He lights up when he can play, hike and camp by himself or with others.

JJ recharges by working out. She's happiest when she engages in physical activity for two hours a day, and she schedules it into her calendar without compromise.

Heather and Colleen radiate joy racing down the slopes. They are both amazing skiers, and bonding with family during their favorite pastime makes for a heavenly experience.

Terry enjoys the movies, sharing his wickedly funny sense of humor over a strong cup of Irish tea and making memories with family.

Debbie loves travel and planning interesting trips to enjoy with her loved ones.

When I reflect on my own life, I see that my most memorable moments of joy occur when I'm laughing, challenging myself physically and being silly with family and friends. I've always been an athlete and pushed myself to participate in marathons, adventure races, triathlons, mountain bike races, ski and snowboard trips and more.

I say participate, because for me, the goal is not to take first place. It is generally to challenge myself, enjoy the company of like-minded individuals and have fun along the way.

For my two marathons, I prioritized fun during both the training and the main event. Throughout my training, I deepened relationships by logging miles with cousins, friends and new connections.

My love of nature and the open road inspired me to run outside. Treadmills make me feel like I'm on a hamster wheel, so it didn't matter the weather; rain, snow, heatwave or shine, I took to the streets.

The long, sometimes grueling runs provided a ton of quality bonding time. Camaraderie naturally occurs when you share a common goal of accomplishing your weekly miles and staying injury-free. You'd be surprised by the level of intimacy that grows when you're processing whatever "stuff" comes up and realize that you're not alone.

On marathon race days, I had two simple goals: Run, and stop to say hello to any friends or family who came out to cheer me on. I didn't prioritize "my finishing time,"

MARY TESS ROONEY

only that I finished and had the privilege of celebrating my accomplishment with my fans along the way.

The New York City marathon is a mega-event, so there were tons of fans I didn't know that I appreciated too. I was energized by the almost thirty personal fans who committed to cheering me on. I had cheered on many other NYC marathoners, so I knew that the encouragement of spectators was an essential part of the momentum. I also knew that mapping routes, coordinating times and navigating the crowds to cheer on your loved ones was like completing an adventure race of your own. I used my visit with my own loved ones as a water break and giggled at whatever they or I was experiencing that day.

For one race, JJ got four massive, gold letter helium balloons that, when combined, spelled MARY so I could easily spot my tribe in the crowds. Of course, they took turns holding the individual balloons so that sometimes the order of the balloons looked more like ARMY, but I still knew they were my people, ha.

I loved finding my family and friends along the route so much that for one marathon, I turned around and ran against the sea of runners to find my mom and aunts when I realized I must have passed them. Yes, many thought I was cray-cray for retracing my steps and adding distance to the 26.2-mile feat, but I knew I'd be more disappointed in not saying hi to Mom before I crossed the finish line.

My priority was fun and family, so going back was my choice. Of course, when I found Mom, she promptly asked me why I was coming from the wrong direction. We both laughed when I told her I wasn't finishing without seeing her first.

Looking back, it's funny that my priority included running in the wrong direction if warranted.

SCHEDULE JOYTIME

Hopefully, by now, you've realized that you work hard every day and need to prioritize fun in everything you do. In addition, consider making a commitment to schedule joytime for yourself and your loved ones.

Joytime is akin to playtime for kids. Kids have playdates and playtime scheduled in as a typical part of their life. This is accepted and even cherished.

Well, in my humble opinion, adults should have joydates and joytime too. Channel your inner child and play more. Your life's journey will be all the richer and sweeter as you weave joytime into your calendar.

When my coaching client, Blake, was going through a big life transition at home and at work, I agreed that we could schedule our calls on a week-to-week basis. The intended goal was to offer flexibility and support him through his transition. The additional benefit we gained was that our text exchanges to secure a date and time opened Blake's mind to how I prioritize fun and schedule joytime in my days.

On one call, Blake admitted that my outside interests and self-care commitments inspired him. Surprised, I asked him to elaborate.

Blake said, "Well, because I currently text you last-minute to ask to chat, I've gotten more familiar with your life outside of our one-on-one meetings. For example, on Monday nights, you go to Drum Circle. You exercise on the beach every morning. You honor time to work on your podcast every day, and you enjoy it."

His comments energized my soul. I really had shifted my priorities and was demonstrating the life I was empowering others to lead!

I had a brief flashback to my former corporate roles, where I took on a ton of additional responsibility and lost a ton of nights and weekends in the process. I beamed with pride, knowing I had completely changed my patterns and learned the art of prioritizing fun, scheduling joytime and elevating my joy frequency. It had made an impression on Blake, and it made one on me, too.

The key is to take time to self-reflect and honor something that brings *you* joy.

MARY TESS ROONEY

Whether you decide to run, paint, knit, write, travel, walk, sing, read, sleep, bird-watch or spend time with loved ones, do it unapologetically.

According to Jessica Cassity's Happify article (September 18, 2014), "Happiness by the Numbers: 8 Stats That Could Change Your Life,"[9] people who regularly spend about a quarter of their hours each day with family and friends are twelve times as likely to report feeling joyful instead of stressed or anxious. Cassity references a June 5, 2008 Gallup poll by Jim Harter and Raksha Arora that revealed that happiness and enjoyment patterns peak on the weekends when we have more time to socialize and play. If spending time with our loved ones brings us joy and makes us happy, what would it feel like to schedule more joytime during the week and not just on the weekends?

PRESENCE OVER PRESENTS

In my family, I'm an open-minded, adventurous, silly and fun daughter, sister, niece, cousin and aunt. I want everyone to feel loved and free to wave their freak flag, if they want. It upsets me when anyone feels pressure to act a certain way or behave according to societal expectations. It took time for me to really embrace my creative, fun-loving side, but I enjoy inspiring others to let their freak flag fly too, or at minimum prioritize fun for themselves.

To help set an example, one of my favorite joytime activities is planning parties and events for loved ones. I love thinking about themes and silly ways to bring out everyone's inner child. Making memories, complete with swag, lights me up. It's a creative guilty pleasure of mine, and I'm good at it. Or at least, my momma tells me so all the time. Ha.

I have the ability to make the attendees laugh and experience their own joytime as a result of my event planning, and that energizes my soul. I'm not big into presents, but I see the joytime experience as the best gift I could offer. I strive to create memorable bonding experiences that will create deeper connections, inspire laughter and result in stories that last a lifetime. In my family, we don't do presents for birthdays. We celebrate by having loved ones' presence encircling the celebration.

Below, I share a few of the "offbeat," silly ways I've honored my three fabulous siblings, Colleen, Heather and JJ. I share them only to reinforce that, in addition to creating joytime for yourself, you can gift it to others, too.

It's critical to remember that life is not meant to be taken seriously all the time. I use milestone birthdays or significant events as welcome opportunities to elevate our joy frequency and create fun, bonding memories in the process.

The bottom line is to prioritize fun, enjoy the experience and cherish the memories you are creating. Your legacy is defined by how you show up for yourself and those who surround you.

GODDESS PARTY

For Colleen's fiftieth birthday, my mom, JJ, Heather and I hosted a party dedicated to channeling our own inner goddesses and remembering all the strong women and goddesses who came before us.

We used Ann Shen's book *Legendary Ladies: 50 Goddesses to Empower and Inspire You*[10] as a conversation starter. My mom and three sisters each selected a goddess (or several goddesses) who resonated with us, and chatted about our own goddess-worthy strengths and abilities.

Like all goddesses, we have each overcome obstacles and adversity to follow our path and make significant contributions to this world. Like all goddesses, we are strong and fearless in our pursuit of the best for ourselves, our loved ones and the world at large.

I made them simple flower crowns. Mine was a little bolder, because why not take advantage of any occasion to wear flowers on my head? We pulled angel and other oracle cards to inspire joyful conversation, recall fond memories, share our dreams and giggle in this safe, loving space.

Most of us are conditioned to be serious and practical during our day jobs, so it can be difficult to switch gears, relax and let our guard down after hours. My mom, my sisters and I share a special bond, but we still have to work at staying connected thanks to our diverse interests and life choices.

We all truly want the best for each other, so it's easy to create a safe space. There are no hidden agendas. The goddess theme was a nice, chill opportunity to recharge, relate and remember what matters most.

WARRIOR DASH

Heather's fortieth birthday was commemorated by a Warrior Dash on Windham Mountain in New York. We had over twenty family members sign up for Red Frog's thrill-seeking event that tests participants' physical and mental stamina as they run 3.2 miles up and down the ski mountain and through thirteen different obstacles including mud trenches, cargo nets, barbed wire and firepits.

My sister Heather is not exactly the "Let's run through mud and over fire for fun" kind of gal, but we had such a great turnout to celebrate her, totaling fifty family members between warrior racers and spectators, that I still see her laughing as we navigated the extremely steep terrain and physical challenges.

What's even cooler is that her kids, Logan and Michaela, still comment on the photos of her leaping over the flames. And the younger generation still talks about how their parents, aunts and uncles slogged or tiptoed through mud pits to avoid the barbed wire.

It lights me up to hear these stories come up in conversation and the laughter sparked by other random memories from that weekend adventure. Pure joytime!

TREASURE HUNT

Another fun event in our family occurred for JJ's fortieth birthday. I created a Treasure Hunt for adults and kids in Brigantine, New Jersey that I branded #JJisOurTreasure. I made up the rules, divided the group into three teams and provided eight rhyming clues that each team had to decipher.

Once the team successfully determined the clue location, they had to visit the site and memorialize it with a fun photo of the family wearing the provided props. For example, one of the clues was to visit the local fire station and take pictures with the ladder or engine crew.

Moons ago, my uncle Terry was a FDNY fireman and fire marshal, so I visited the Brigantine firehouse prior to the event to see if the crew would play along and wear fake mustaches for a laugh. Of course, so long as duty doesn't call, firemen are always game to prioritize fun, so they were engaged, entertaining and amazing sports!

The non-timed event focused on fun and family bonding. Mom and I made rice krispie treats (JJ's favorite), wrapped and branded as 40K gold bars, which were the treasure once everyone solved all the riddles and completed all the photo opportunities. And yes, everyone was a winner, because the purpose was quality joytime and laughter, and that was accomplished in spades.

CHECKPOINT: PRIORITIZE FUN AND ELEVATE YOUR JOY FREQUENCY

As you reflect, notice your emotional responses. Each heart-centered feeling that surfaces provides clues that will influence your choices and inform your actions.

MARY TESS ROONEY

Instrumental Insights

- ~ The more fun and Heart Value alignment there is in your life, the more joy you will experience. This energetic vibration elevates and grows as you channel more joy.

- ~ Work-life balance is a unicorn; prioritize fun in all you do for harmony.

- ~ Companies mean well, but it's up to you to actually implement change. You don't need a company's approval to prioritize fun or infuse balance into your life.

WISE WALK REFLECTION

Journal without judgment and process these Wise Walk questions to gain awareness.

1. How does the idea of prioritizing fun make you feel? Does it make you cringe because you pride yourself on being a hard worker? Or does it feel appealing and possible?

2. What choices are available to you so that you can combine work and enjoyment like Collin and I did (discussing business while running in Central Park)?

3. What's one action you will commit to this week to prioritize fun and elevate your joy frequency?

FEEL-CHOOSE-ACT AMPLIFIER

Observe an area in your life that you'd like to address and apply this feel, choose and act amplifier. Jump right in, or read the following examples to get your Feel-Choose-Act juices flowing.

Feel	Choose	Act

Feel > Choose > Act

Feel	Choose	Act
I wanted to feel energized and supported by creating a connection with my NYC marathon fans (aka friends and family).	I made a choice to stop every time I saw a friend or family member and chat for a little to create a shared memory. I made a choice not to be concerned with my finishing time.	When I accidently passed my mom near the finish line, I turned around (adding extra distance) and ran back to see her because I knew my choice would energize me.

MARY TESS ROONEY

Affirmation

I prioritize fun and experience joy, every day.

Tip:

Instead of asking, "What did you *do* today?" start asking your loved ones, "In what ways did you have *fun* today?" Or, " How did you *prioritize fun* today?"

Notes:

Get Your Stride On

Take the time to brainstorm ways to prioritize fun in your daily activities so it doesn't become an afterthought.

MARY TESS ROONEY

Endnotes

Jennifer Blake, "The 30 Greatest Places to Work For This Year (That are All Hiring Right Now!)," TheMuse.com, last accessed June 15, 2021, https://www.themuse.com/advice/30-greatest-companies-to-work-for-this-year-that-are-all-hiring-right-now

5

6   Nick Davidson, "The 50 Best Places to Work in 2019," OutsideOnline.com, November 4, 2019, https://www.outsideonline.com/2404274/best-places-to-work-2019.

7   Tidying Up with Marie Kondo, Netflix, 2019, https://www.netflix.com/title/80209379.

8   Julia Cameron, *The Artist's Way* (New York: TarcherPerigee, 1992), p. 18.

9   Jessica Cassity, "Happiness by the Numbers: 8 Stats That Could Change Your Life," Happify.com, last accessed June 15, 2021, https://www.happify.com/hd/happiness-by-the-numbers/.

10   Ann Shen, *Legendary Ladies: 50 Goddesses to Empower and Inspire You* (San Francisco: Chronicle Books, 2018).

CHAPTER 7

DIRECT YOUR PATH: CHOOSE YOUR OWN ADVENTURE

What we focus on takes root, grows and expands. Our mind is so powerful, it emits a frequency that, if channeled, will set things in motion.

My family loves the outdoors and staying active. My sisters, cousins and I were raised to use our minds and muscles to overcome extreme challenges, so when we discovered an adventure race that incorporated orienteering, running, mountain biking, canoeing and team challenges, we said, "Heck yes, let's do it!"

We promptly signed up two teams of three ladies each. My cousins Debbie, Kathryn and I were on one team, and my sister JJ and her childhood friends, Martha and Abby, were on the other team. Six months prior to the race, JJ's firstborn child, Avery, came into this world, so my brother-in-law Matty and other fathers watched the kiddos and tailgated while the ladies hit the trails.

It turned out to be a beautiful day, and we were all excited to explore the mountains of Pennsylvania. None of us had ever been to this particular state park, so being there was an adventure in itself. As we chatted, we overheard other teams assigning roles and strategizing.

I remember thinking, "Is that level of detail really necessary?" I could tell by the questioning look Debbie and Kathryn had on their faces that we were all thinking the same thing. As our eyes met, we burst out laughing and said, "We'll be fine, right? We'll just wing it?"

That thought was quickly interrupted by a voice abruptly telling us to pipe down. The race director held the megaphone to his lips and barked at us, "Move closer! We can't begin until I review the race rules and the racer code of conduct."

Wow, this was feeling very official.

He began with, "Each race team must complete the race as directed. Each team will be assigned a specific course sequence to follow." He went on, "As a team, you will stick together and advance as a unit. And the only equipment you are approved to use is your map and a compass."

In case you were wondering, "using a compass" does *not* mean using your smartphone's compass or some other GPS device. The only approved compass was old-school, so we had a baseplate compass with magnetic arrows ready to go.

The race director continued, "There are volunteers manning all transition areas to ensure that you follow your course map, and they will randomly verify your progress and compliance with each phase."

We hadn't received our course map yet, so this instruction didn't mean much at the

MARY TESS ROONEY

time, but we began to realize that adventure racers and race directors had an approach that was very different from our typical, let's show up and run a 5K style. This crew was serious.

The race director continued, "At each checkpoint, your team must record proof of visitation, which means you will use the hole punch at that checkpoint to punch your card and mark that checkpoint as complete."

We nodded our heads in agreement. Okay, that seemed pretty straightforward.

Then he got very serious and stern. His hands gestured toward the medical and search and rescue teams standing by. "Our top priorities, for everyone today, are to have fun and be safe...again, have fun and be safe."

Then he began to bark again. "This racecourse has a concrete six-hour time limit, which means you need to pay attention to your time and, as you get close to the six-hour time cap, wherever you are on this mountain, you need to hightail it back to base and check in with one of these volunteers to report that you are safe. This is nonnegotiable, and we have no tolerance for any racer who does not follow this requirement. And yes, checking in is imperative because if you forget, and we cannot account for your where-abouts, we will have to assume that you are still on the mountain. And we will deploy our search and rescue teams to retrieve you."

I couldn't help but wonder, "Has that really ever happened?" Followed by, "Okay, can we start now?"

Thankfully, the rules and code of conduct portion was over. The organizers gave each team a race packet outlining our specific challenges and route.

Our team's race sequence, in order, was team challenges, mountain bike, run and canoe. Again, per the rules, we had to successfully navigate and acquire hole punches in one event, like mountain biking, before we could move on to the next, like running. Debbie, Kathryn and I checked in with each other. Our goal was simple: Collect all the checkpoint punches way before the six-hour time limit. We were physically fit and resourceful, so finishing seemed doable.

The team challenges were mentally and physically demanding, but not impossible. We scaled and descended a rope net, like the Army uses for training. We walked across two high beams that veered out at increasing angles of difficulty while pressing against each other's hands for leverage because we were not allowed to touch the ground.

We surfaced a ping-pong ball that was lodged at the bottom of a five-foot, perforated PVC pipe. This was the most time-consuming challenge for us, but we got the ball to float to the top by plugging the pipe's holes with our hands, legs—whatever we had—as we filled the pipe with water. We successfully tackled a few other team challenges, all in lockstep, because we could not advance unless all of us completed the activity together.

Our teamwork, hustle and can-do spirit paid off. The race director's rules seemed easy, and we were on track to complete the entire adventure race well before the six-hour time limit.

After team challenges, we huddled and looked at the map before we set out on our mountain bikes. The remaining events required "orienteering" skills and we weren't even novice map readers.

As we stared at the map, one of us asked the question on all of our minds. "What's the deal with all those squiggly lines?"

Wait, they indicate steep inclines as they get closer together, you say?!? Yikes, the whole map was tight, squiggly lines. What were we thinking?

This should have been our first clue to reassess our strategy, but we still agreed: "There's no way it will take us longer than six hours." I hadn't learned to read the signs yet, so, true to our play by the rules upbringing, we forged ahead.

Consequently, what should have been a fifteen-mile bike ride ended up being closer to thirty-plus miles. What should have been a five-mile run took us over ten miles

MARY TESS ROONEY

(hahaha). We had our compass, but I am not sure we used it—at least, not effectively.

We kept getting off course (aka lost) and had to backtrack, bushwhack or worse, cross a deep river carrying our mountain bikes over our heads to acquire a checkpoint mark. That river, by the way, was pure sludge at the bottom. We sank in mud up to our calves and squealed loudly as we waded through waist-high water and gross muck to get to the other side. Yucky and exhausting.

My sister JJ's team started off with the same simple goal: Collect all the checkpoint markers before the six-hour time limit. They even had Martha, a map smarty-pants who knew what those squiggly lines in close proximity meant.

They too started off strong with the team challenges, and as they moved into their next event, which was running, they quickly realized that they craved a different experience and outcome, so their team goals shifted mid-experience. As a new mom, JJ wanted exercise and to have fun with Abby and Martha while their husbands were on childcare duty. Midstream, they decided, "Who cares if we collect all those checkpoint markers or not?"

Meanwhile, Debbie, Kathryn and I plugged along and tackled each event according to the rules and our original objectives. We were competitive and had a lot of laughs at our own expense.

We completed every team challenge, the mountain bike, and all of the running within the six hours; but we never made it to the canoe portion, so we ended up with a big ol' DNF. If you don't know what DNF means…oh yeah, it's DID NOT FINISH.

DNF in adventure race lingo is short for Did Not Finish and means we did not collect all the required checkpoint markers within the time limit.

Notes:

When we returned to our spectators and crew hanging out on the lawn with beers, JJ, Abby and Martha were completely relaxed. When I asked JJ when they finished, she said casually, "Oh, a while ago."

Impressed, I said, "Wow, you guys are awesome! We had such a hard time orienteering and navigating the best route to collect all those checkpoint marks that we didn't even make it to the canoe."

JJ laughed wholeheartedly and replied, "Oh no, we didn't try to get all those checkpoints. We got several for each event, and when we had enough, we moved on to the next activity. We knew we wouldn't win, so we decided to enjoy some tailgate time too."

DUH! Leave it to my little sister to teach me that adventures are meant to be enjoyed, and it's okay to make up your own rules for how you direct your path.

None of us were in it to win it. We were all first-time adventure racers. None of us had trained, acquired the necessary skills or set realistic goals to successfully compete.

Debbie, Kathryn and I, while physically fit, lacked basic map skills and had zero knowledge of that particular mountain, so we couldn't even fake it. We didn't stop to reconsider if the rules aligned with what we wanted from the experience, nor change our approach when the signs appeared. We relied on our determination and competitive nature to push us from one checkpoint to the next, until we literally ran out of time six hours later.

My team and I had a blast, and it's such a great memory for me that I feel like we did win. Plus, our DNF served as a great life lesson in directing our path based on grounded, realistic and attainable goals. With a little preparation, our adventure race outcome would have been EPIC (envision, plan, implement and cherish), but you'll learn all about that approach in the next chapter.

It was also refreshing to know that no one thought less of JJ, Abby and Martha for making up their own rules. In fact, in that moment, as my strained legs wobbled from

MARY TESS ROONEY

six hours of steep inclines, I admired them immensely for accepting their beginner status and directing their path according to their inner compass and joy.

DIRECT YOUR PATH

CHOOSE YOUR OWN ADVENTURE INSPIRATION

If you've ever read a *Choose Your Own Adventure*® book, you know that each story is written in the second person to allow the reader (aka you) to immerse yourself in the plot and be the main character. The author creates a scenario and sets the stage. You, as the protagonist, read along until you are presented with two or three options to select to continue your adventure.

I didn't read a ton of *Choose Your Own Adventure*® books, but when I did, I seemed to enjoy science fiction stories where I, as the lead character, encountered a supernatural phenomenon. The fate of the world rested in my hands as I decided whether the occurrence was caused by a ghost from the afterlife, aliens from outer space or an earthbound prankster who created an illusion of the paranormal.

Murder mysteries, medieval royal conspiracies and time travel intrigues also fascinated me. Whether I was the head detective or a kid who stumbled upon a portal and traveled back in time, I relished the authority to steer my heroine's direction and the actions of the unfolding storyline.

While the *Choose Your Own Adventure*® series was pure fantasy, and some had bizarre twists, I always felt empowered to explore the possibility that resonated with me most and choose that path. I knew my *pick-a-path* decisions led to yet more decisions, until I chose one possible ending.

The other cool aspect was knowing that I always had the freedom to choose again. If I read a couple pages and didn't like the narrative, I had permission to return to the previous fork in the road and voilà, I was headed in a different direction.

The uncertainty, intrigue and adventure of these books are much like real life. Life is unpredictable. It's common to encounter crossroads, unexpected outcomes and detours on any given path. The key is to embrace where you are and where you want to go, and have the courage to explore the twists and turns as they present themselves. Or be willing to navigate forward or backward, figuratively speaking, if your decisions don't turn out as planned.

I'm not suggesting you can erase history. That's not possible. However, we can learn from each adventure and we can, to some degree, proactively design or reactively reroute to create a more desirable experience.

YOUR FOCUS BECOMES REALITY

As Mom says, "Thoughts are things." What we focus on takes root, grows and expands. Our minds are so powerful, they emit a frequency that, if channeled, will set things in motion.

Your Heart Value is your power charge! The key is to carefully gear your thoughts toward desired outcomes and visualize that state of being.

Note, I say drive toward *outcomes*, not deadlines, because sometimes it may take longer than we'd like. Sometimes our self-imposed deadlines help us focus our efforts. That's a reality, but we shouldn't overlook progress or lose sight of how we will *feel* once we finally arrive.

MARY TESS ROONEY

If the adventure race didn't have a time limit, I'm almost positive Debbie, Kathryn and I would have finished. We cared more about the complete experience and feeling accomplished than the time associated with our effort.

If the adventure theme doesn't resonate with you, consider pursuing your *something* like a treasure hunt. Your joy, happiness and health are the best rewards you can hunt and discover for yourself.

As you know, I love treasure hunts. JJ's fortieth birthday, #JJisOurTreasure, was a blast. Treasure hunts and maps are a hit in our family because it's an easy way to keep the kids entertained while they use problem-solving skills and teamwork to search for clues and have fun. My uncle Joe still creates treasure maps for the younger generations in our family, and watching their personal self-discovery is awesome.

Also, one of my favorite movies is *The Goonies*[11]. If you haven't seen *The Goonies*, you need to!! It's a classic for all ages about misunderstood kids who find a treasure map and pursue fortune in the hopes of preventing foreclosure on their parents' homes.

The Goonies band together to follow the clues, cross paths with challenges (including some bad dudes) and experience some proud moments of self-realization along the way. At first, they may be misunderstood kids, but they follow their hearts, hunt for what they want and ultimately discover treasure in uplifting and unexpected ways.

I don't want to spoil the ending for you, but what's relevant to you as you read this book is that every time you choose your own adventure, your self-awareness, self-confidence and self-worth will grow exponentially. What's also significant is how self-realization and owning your unique value leads to deeper bonds and stronger heart-centered relationships.

Once you learn who you are and what you truly treasure, like the Goonies, your ability to offer value that lights you up grows. When your thoughts focus on energetic and emotional connections, those synchronicities become more frequent because your heart-centered vibration attracts what you seek. For example, if you hunt for what energizes you, you'll attract more invigorating experiences. Then you'll have more energy to discover and hunt what fuels you.

On the flip side, if you vibrate negative thoughts or feelings, you'll attract low-vibration experiences and people. Each time you make an investment in you, you gain powerful awareness of what makes your heart happy or depletes you—so protect your thoughts. Then feel, choose and act with intention. Your thoughts become your reality.

PICK-A-PATH TO POWER YOUR HEART VALUE

Now that your amazing and compelling Value Vault is complete, it's time to use your past and present insights to strategically advise your future. Your Value Vault is critical to staying grounded in what you want to *feel* as you intentionally direct your path.

What's possible when you decide to live by your Heart Value rules and *choose your own adventure*? What does success on your own terms look and feel like? What pick-a-paths are calling you? Where do you want to go?

Remember Rocky, the easygoing data manager in his late thirties whose four-page, bulleted Value Vault illuminated his Heart Value and passions surrounding guitar and writing? When he and I first met, he was deflated, miserable and ready to give his two-week notice. Post-Value Vault exercise, Rocky's urgent desire to quit his job dissipated. He felt empowered with new insights and motivated to follow his heart. Instead of running away, he saw the opportunity to design his best adventure.

When I asked Rocky to envision his long- and short-term feelings, he gave me a list of things he *didn't* want to experience. His funk had trained his brain to see problems and he was clearer on what he *didn't want* in life than what he *did*.

That happens to us all from time to time. It's okay to acknowledge those negative themes, but it's important to commit to reframing those thoughts into the positive feelings and experiences you *do* want to create. Otherwise, you'll keep attracting the negative because that's all your brain hears.

Rocky reframed his desired visualization from *not feeling* exhausted, fogged, stuck and cranky, to *feeling* uninhibited, clear, creative, strong and happy. He shifted his mind-set to refrain from bad habits that depleted his mental clarity and limited his creative potential. Instead, he fueled consistent choices that stimulated his confidence, power, fulfillment and self-love.

In working with professionals with various levels of experience, and actually anyone who feels unappreciated, at work or at home, I've discovered that the desire to feel more valued usually translates to four main areas: *confidence, visibility, joy frequency* and *earning potential.* To help Rocky brainstorm action steps to ignite his new direction, he used the *pick-a-path* exercise (Bonus Adventure 6 at the back of this book) to select *choices* and *actions* to help him achieve his feeling goals.

Rocky chose to increase confidence and build his self-belief as his main theme. Instead of focusing on changing jobs, he wanted to explore his passions for guitar and writing while taking actions to improve his mental and physical health. Since the pick-a-path exercise is about seeing, defining and progressing, he detailed specific behaviors to execute weekly in order to achieve his goal of *feeling* clear, creative, strong, uninhibited and happy.

For Rocky, that meant asking his friend Marco, a talented fitness trainer, for support. He committed to daily workouts and an eating regimen based on Marco's guidance. Rocky and Marco met weekly to discuss progress, celebrate wins and modify his plan based on next-level goals. With a few weeks of discipline, Rocky felt mentally and physically strong, energized and more confident.

He also made traction toward feeling creative, happy and fulfilled. Rocky started a side hustle teaching guitar lessons to beginners, and blocked out time on his calendar to create new songs. Rocky followed Julia Cameron's *The Artist's Way*[12] advice by incorporating the morning pages and artist dates into his life. The morning pages are "three pages of longhand writing, strictly stream-of-consciousness" journal entries written every morning. He used Julia's tools—the morning pages and scheduling a weekly artist date with himself—to nurture his creativity. His commitment to journaling and artist dates unlocked his passions and natural talents. Weeks later, he realized that his morning pages had morphed into a creative outlet for fiction. With some reflection, he acknowledged his desire to write a science fiction and fantasy book for people who enjoy mystical characters and medieval battles.

In four months, Rocky went from feeling miserable and stuck to feeling energized and inspired. He's still working at the same job, but his renewed focus on what lights him up makes his work feel more acceptable. His increased confidence and progress toward his passions of writing a book, offering guitar lessons and feeling fit raised his joy frequency to a point where the job frustrations were no longer important.

Now, it's your turn. I understand you've already invested a ton of time and attention in your Value Vault and emotional contrast responses. Those exercises are the foundation for you to be aware, clear and have more choice in how you live your best life.

Your life is an adventure, and you are reading this book for a reason. Perhaps you are feeling unappreciated at work and want a raise or a promotion. You are tired of letting others take the credit for your hard work, so you need to speak up and skillfully promote your contributions. Perhaps you are working with a new boss who doesn't appreciate your Heart Value and it's shaken your confidence, but you are ready to get it back. Maybe you want to experience more joy and have the courage to go after the life you crave.

Perhaps you seek personal fulfillment and more time with activities, friends and connections that light you up. Or maybe you see your children struggling with the difference between validation and appreciation. You want to set a good example for them and see their Heart Value cherished in the way they deserve.

Regardless of your why, now is your time to choose your own adventure and pick what path or paths you intend to venture on. In working with coaching clients of all ages, I've noted that the desire to increase confidence, visibility, joy and earning potential are common goals.

Increase Your . . .

Confidence

Visibility

Joy Frequency

Earning Potential

Let's say you want to *increase confidence*. There's a big aspect of self-study to build your self-belief. Here are some pick-a-path ideas some of my clients applied to feel more confident: develop your expertise; maintain a positive mindset; gain awareness; engage a mentor; update headshots; improve self-care through health-related, social and emotional actions; improve public speaking; do something for the first time; define your personal brand statement; become an influencer; and more. The ways to increase your Heart Value expertise are endless.

Or maybe your main goal is to *increase visibility*. My client Bobby committed to four tactics in support of this goal: he served on committees, volunteered for special projects, built his network and submitted his name to be a panelist or speaker at industry events. Other clients selected two or three other visibility goals related to a marketing plan and objectives; public relations or social media activities like becoming a newsletter or blog contributor; requesting to be a guest on podcasts; and more.

Let's pretend that what you want most is to *increase your earning potential*. One strategy that you now know is to build your worth by voicing your Value Vault.

Edith realized that she had reached her maximum earning level; she needed to create a transition plan and exit strategy. Another client, Max, decided to ask for a raise and used his Value Vault in combination with market research and his company's competency criteria to justify his pay increase. Other common ideas are to consider requesting a bonus increase or other financial incentives. You can also earn more money by having a side hustle or developing new abilities that make you more marketable.

The best ideas for how you choose your own adventure are within you, based on how you want to support your dream attainment.

If you want some prompts for brainstorming what direction you want to choose, review the pick-a-path ideas in Bonus Adventure 6 related to increasing confidence, visibility, joy and earning potential. Notice the ideas that speak to your heart. Write down new possible paths that call to you but aren't listed yet.

MARY TESS ROONEY

Pay attention to your physical responses *on a cellular level*. Which ideas excite or energize you? If you are drawn to an activity, say *yes*! You have the ability (or will attract the resources) to tackle any and all of them. Don't let limiting beliefs or self-doubt stop you!

Remember, the choice to *do nothing* is also an action. This is your opportunity to intentionally move forward in the direction that serves *you*. Be willing to design new opportunities and accept new challenges. I guarantee that if you take one step, and then another, you will hit your True Stride and find a fulfilling groove.

The key is to honor your *feelings*, explore your options, take action and trust the process! As long as you take aligned Heart Value action, there is no right or wrong way to proceed. Energy, support and resources will surface as you put this practice in motion and blaze your trail! This is *your* adventure. Have fun with it and reap increased fortitude, appreciation and worth as a result!

DON'T GIVE UP OR DNF

Georgia's Heart Value connected deeply with the fitness and wellness industry. She paid the bills as a training manager working for a software service company, but on the side, she organized weight training competitions and coached participants in nutrition and exercise.

Georgia's Value Vault, a bulleted two-page outline, showcased her proudest moments of helping her gym buddies achieve a fitness goal or set a personal record. Her cringeworthy moments were when she started but didn't finish something; she dropped out of college to work for the family business with only a few remaining courses left, and started two separate health related-businesses with friends that started strong but then fizzled out.

When Georgia shared her vision, I was surprised by her lofty expectations of herself. She already had a full-time job and family obligations on her plate. I was unclear where she'd find the extra time in her schedule to tackle the seven additional action items—with three-plus subsets each week—to increase her confidence and visibility. From my perspective, her ambitious vision, given the other demands on her time, seemed unrealistic.

If, like Georgia, you have a past pattern where you excitedly bite off more than you can chew and then run out of steam, please give yourself permission to start small and gain early wins. Take it from someone who has gotten a DNF: Set yourself up for success before you step into action. While you don't have a time cap for when you arrive at your desired outcome, you will quit of your own accord—or worse, get injured—if you can't sustain your stride to the finish line.

In one of my former corporate roles, I deployed enterprise-wide systems and software like intranets and client relationship management tools. When a project began to suffer from scope creep, which happened naturally, I'd ask individuals, teams and project owners to review each item on the project enhancement list and decide if the requirement was "mission critical" or a "personal preference."

This transparent dialogue accomplished three goals. One, it gave the owner the freedom to choose again. Perhaps initially an item was mission critical, but among eighty other priorities it could easily be redefined as personal preference. Two, clarity on mission-critical items got teams focused on the essentials. A more manageable and realistic plan supercharged teams and produced quicker big and small wins. Three, I found it helpful to uncover shiny objects (aka nice-to-haves) and cut through the noise (opinions and pressure from outside expectations).

When I asked Georgia how she intended to manage the various time commitments and competing priorities, she could not answer. When I asked her to review each planned action and clarify if her choice was "mission critical or a personal preference," only twenty percent of her items surfaced as mission critical.

MARY TESS ROONEY

Do you know what becomes possible when you transparently evaluate what priorities require your energy, resources and time? Your chances of success increase exponentially when you eliminate the "personal preference" items in favor of your "mission critical" goals. You are less distracted by the nice-to-have items and are freed up to execute on what really matters. It's invigorating to see a plan distilled down to its essence, and move from a dreamy vision to a realistic and achievable plan.

REFRAME LIMITATIONS TO SUCCEED

The limiting beliefs below may weigh you down and restrict your progress if left unaddressed. Rewire your mindset so they don't overpower the adventure.

Limiting Belief	Reframe Belief	Reality
Not sure where to start	If it feels intimidating at first, that's normal. Start small and keep it simple. Choose one goal with an attainable weekly milestone to direct your path and get you moving in the right direction. Get a buddy and set up an accountability exchange.	The choice to do nothing is an action too. If you don't try to envision, plan and prepare, you won't be any closer to what your heart desires.
Not enough time to plan and prepare	Review essentials, reprioritize and find the time for you!	The time you take to plan and prepare before the action phase will minimize frustration and save you more time in the long run.

Limiting Belief	Reframe Belief	Reality
Fear of going down the wrong path	Remember, it is normal to reroute or change paths. This means you are trusting your inner compass and choosing to move forward aligned with your Heart Value.	This is your plan, so you have the complete authority to adjust, redirect or pause at any time.
Fear of disappointing others	There's an opportunity cost and price to pay for allowing others to direct your path.	It's time to live your life according to your own inner compass and joy. The benefits far outweigh any perceived negatives. This mindful shift, from seeking approval externally to honoring your Heart Value internally, will increase your freedom and fulfillment.
Still unclear on my direction	Pick one tactic. Start small and pay attention to what surfaces as you proceed. Envision, plan, implement, cherish… and repeat.	Your plan is a living document that will change over time. Review, update and celebrate the plan often to stay accountable and on track to achieve your goals and objectives.

Once you outline your priorities, you will continue to fuel your feelings, choices and actions to gain momentum. Many roadblocks may stand in your way, but typically, there's a way to move forward—if you mentally prepare and show up with that intention. You have come this far. Have faith that you can go the distance!

CHECKPOINT: CHOOSE YOUR ADVENTURE

As you reflect, notice your emotional responses. Each heart-centered feeling that surfaces provides clues that will influence your choices and inform your actions.

Instrumental Insights

- Pay attention, on a cellular level, to paths that excite or energize you. If you are drawn to an activity, say yes! You have the ability (or will attract the resources) to tackle any and all of them. Don't let limiting beliefs or self-doubt prevent you!

- The *choice* to *do nothing* is an action. Be willing to design new opportunities, accept new challenges and *take one step*, and then *another*…until you hit your True Stride and find a fulfilling groove.

- There is no right or wrong way to proceed as long as you take aligned *Heart Value* action.

- This is *your* adventure. Have fun with it and reap increased fortitude, appreciation, fun and worth as a result!

WISE WALK REFLECTION

Journal without judgment and process these Wise Walk questions to gain awareness.

1. As you look ahead, what paths energize and excite you? Are you mindlessly collecting checkpoint markers without realizing how you want to feel throughout the experience?

2. From someone who has gotten a DNF, will the choices you are making set you up for success? If you accidently bit off more than you can chew, will you give yourself permission to choose a new path?

3. Do you take time to evaluate your *mission-critical* actions versus your personal preferences? What's one *personal preference* action you will let go of this week to make space for your mission-critical items?

FEEL-CHOOSE-ACT AMPLIFIER

Observe an area in your life that you'd like to address and apply this feel, choose and act amplifier. Jump right in, or read the following examples to get your Feel-Choose-Act juices flowing.

Feel	Choose	Act

Feel ▶ **Choose** ▶ **Act**

Feel	Choose	Act
My adventure team wanted to feel a sense of accomplishment in finishing our first adventure race.	We made a choice to follow the rules and acquire each checkpoint in the order assigned.	We completed three of the four events until we ran out of time. We implemented our action plan, stayed the course and received a DNF.
JJ's adventure team wanted to have fun and enjoy each other's company.	They made a choice to loosely follow the rules, and they redirected their path when they didn't want to collect any more checkpoints.	They didn't pay attention to the number of checkpoints they collected and also received a DNF, but we all had a blast together.

Affirmation

I will direct my path according to my inner compass and joy.

Tip:

Since the *choice* to *do nothing* is an action, make a choice that gets you closer to your goals. Each time you take steps that align with your heart, you'll expand and find your groove. This is your opportunity to intentionally move forward in the direction that serves you.

Get Your Stride On

Your chances of success increase
exponentially when you eliminate the
"personal preference" items in favor of
your "mission critical" goals. You are less
distracted by the nice-to-have items
and are freed up to execute on
what really matters.

Endnotes

11   Richard Donner, *The Goonies*, Amblin Entertainment, Inc., 1985.

12   Cameron, *The Artist's Way*, p. 9.

MARY TESS ROONEY

CHAPTER 8

DESIGN YOUR EPIC ADVENTURE: ENVISION, PLAN, IMPLEMENT AND CHERISH

I know some people think vision boards are for woo-woo spirit junkies, but there's research to support the effectiveness of envisioning and mapping out your goals.

All the reading, reflecting, documenting and introspection has been leading you to this point: The point where you take your enlightened emotional awareness and design your EPIC adventure. EPIC stands for *Envision, Plan, Implement* and *Cherish*, and is your personal map of where you want to go and the strategies to get there. Be sure to design your adventure with checkpoints to celebrate your progress or change your course along the way.

Unlike most strategic plans in business, you will once again use the *feelings* you want to embody as your target destination. Possessions, like a new car, a house or a watch, are acceptable goals, but belongings themselves won't spark your heart or energize your soul. Quite frankly, material assets are not as impactful or lasting as feelings, either. Too often, people think, "I will be happy once I buy a house." They buy the house, and then the attainment goal shifts to, "I will be happy when I pay off my mortgage." That achievement comes to fruition and the new target becomes, "I will be happy when I buy a bigger house."

Perhaps the purchase of a new home offers security, safety or pride. Those feelings are all relatable. Who doesn't want to feel safe and secure? The house itself can't offer happiness. Happiness is about who you are and how you feel in that house.

As you read this chapter to design your EPIC adventure, I encourage you to really get clear on the underlying feelings you want to embody along the way. Use your feelings as checkpoints or guideposts to ensure that you stay aligned to your real self, each step of the way. Success on your terms is more likely in that frame of mind.

An adventure race is a multi-sport team event in which racers navigate a challenging

MARY TESS ROONEY

course using a map, compass and route strategy within a set time limit. Adventure races require a mix of smarts, stamina, speed and strength. Teammates communicate and compete against others and the clock to move from checkpoint to checkpoint, collecting the markers.

Together, we will use the adventure race metaphor to have fun while you route your paths and objectives toward living your best life. However, this is *not* a race, so the drive is toward outcomes, not deadlines or time limits. There's no need to rush past milestones on your path to discovery.

Your goal is to have an EPIC adventure and *get your stride on*, which represents feelings of fulfilment, joy, purpose or whatever your heart desires. This four-step process, combined with your strategy, smarts, stamina and strength, empowers you to:

Envision where you want to go in life, based on how you want to feel.

Plan your route and paths with a series of checkpoints to help you advance toward your feeling finish line.

Implement your plan using time, energy and resources to support your advancement from start to finish.

Cherish your progress and momentum, and your ability to *choose again* if the road you are traveling no longer resonates with you.

ENVISION

The first step in designing your EPIC adventure is to envision where you want to go and how you want to feel when you arrive.

EPIC, in EPIC adventure, stands for Envision, Plan, Implement and Cherish.

Notes:

As I move through life, I want to feel an energetic and emotional connection with activities, experiences, places and people. If it's not there, it doesn't make the experience, person or place bad; but time is too precious to rationalize or justify a wrong fit. If we are not energetically aligned, then it's okay to mentally thank the experience, encounter or exchange for showing us the disconnect and happily move on. Every living thing deserves to vibrate at a higher frequency and feel appreciated in ways that matter.

With my Value Vault complete, my own long-term goal became to walk in my True Stride and fuel my energy with vibrant adventure, simplicity and laughter, surrounded by people who appreciate my Heart Value. I've made it a practice to trust my inner compass as I envision, plan and prepare.

My short-term milestones focused on how to achieve each feeling of adventure, simplicity and laughter while surrounded by my Heart Value peeps. For simplicity, I wanted the freedom to start my own business and write this book, which meant revamping my cost-of-living structure. To make that possible, I sold my assets in the Northeast and relocated to sunny Florida. My new hometown offers the lifestyle, pace and people that support my fun, outdoorsy and whimsical side.

What is possible when you decide to live by your Heart Value rules and choose your own adventure? What does success on your own terms look like? What is calling to you? Where do you want to go?

As you *envision* your future, think both long-term and short-term. A long-term goal provides clarity on your desired endgame. Short-term milestones allow you to track progress, celebrate forward movement, adjust plans on the fly (with the big picture in mind) and gain momentum. Both provide a strong foundation before you put plans in motion to stride toward your best adventure. And remember, you don't have to capture all the checkpoint markers!

MARY TESS ROONEY

ENVISIONING MEETS AWARENESS, IMAGINATION AND FEAR

I love the envision phase of this process because the only limitations are your own awareness, imagination and fear. There is no price for entry when it comes to envisioning, so dream away!

For decades, I was a vanlife spectator. I admired and followed adventurous free spirits like Kristen Bor, Joe Hawley and others who bravely redefined their priorities and literally hit the road. I even cheered them on when they encountered, and vulnerably shared, their individual bumps in the road.

Following vanlife and vanners was my guilty pleasure and my source of inspiration for a simpler life. While the thought of being a full-time or even a part-time vanner seemed like a massive stretch for me, I couldn't help but dream, research and begin to envision my own camper van essentials.

As a corporate executive, I traveled a ton, but my trips were usually jam-packed with meetings and quick returns to manage other pressing demands at home. While away, I mostly saw the inside of boardrooms and conference facilities. On rare occasions, I'd visit with a friend over dinner, go for a quick run, hike, or hit the slopes. I'd experience enough local flair to mentally add the destination to a "future leisure trip" list.

For over two decades, I consistently prioritized work and nurturing relationships. As I look back, three things stood out as I began to envision how I wanted to feel post-corporate chains.

One, this country's cultural diversity and outdoor grandeur amazes me! My expansive but brief exposure ignited my desire to explore our nation and its majestic national parks with wonderment and awe. I wanted to feel free, unscheduled and connected to nature.

Two, I wanted to laugh with genuine friends across the country and enjoy the relationships we've nurtured. I am grateful for those relationships that took root and grew as we innovated, offered solutions, and made a difference in the communities we served.

Three, my health remained a top priority, which meant that travel needed to support my clean eating and self-care practices.

Since my only limitations were my awareness, imagination and fear, I spent quality time processing each potential emotional trigger before I envisioned what I wanted and how that made me feel.

For awareness, I re-grounded myself in why van life fascinated me. My first insight was that even though I enjoy travel, I consistently miss my own bed and creature comforts while I'm on the road. I need a minimum of seven hours of sleep a night. Travel with a bed in tow, while not uber-practical, sounded dreamy (pun intended) to me.

Staying at a friend or family member's home is always a nice option, but I never want to overstay my welcome or feel like I'm on eggshells if my early to bed, early to rise lifestyle doesn't align with their normal routines.

My mom and I think there's truth to that old joke, "What do fish and houseguests have in common? They both stink after three days." Yes, hardy-har, but kind of true. I appreciate everyone's generosity, and I am also a fan of having my own personal space so I can follow my natural circadian rhythm and routines.

Nourishment—here I mean food, fluids and supplements—is another big consideration for me. My health awareness has led me to follow several nutrition regimens that support and optimize my overall energy, constitution and well-being.

I have eliminated all processed foods, dairy, gluten, soy, caffeine and raw vegetables. I eat organic, sustainably farmed products and grass-fed meats. I follow recipes from the Specific Carbohydrate Diet, which excludes sugar, gluten and other ingredients that inflame the gut.

Hydration is key. I drink a green powder supplement, aloe juice and lemon in my water every morning, along with a probiotic. I enjoy one to two organic juices a day,

MARY TESS ROONEY

either handmade or from a cold press company I trust who ships them frozen. I make one fresh fruit smoothie, sometimes with a nut butter or vegan pea protein powder.

My Berkey water filtration system, Instapot and Vitamix are also part of my nourishment routine. Basically, fueling my body with good, clean, healthy sustenance is key. I find ways to manage my food, fluids and supplements if I'm traveling for less than a week, but my body is not agreeable when I have to relinquish my routine for over a week. Yes, I realize that I sound very high-maintenance. I know that cooking a meal for me probably sounds like a nightmare, too, ha.

In truth, that's how the vision for my mobile lifestyle started. I love visiting family and friends, and exploring nature in all its glory, but not at the expense of my health and sanity.

The other factor is having the ability to work remotely while traveling. I want to visit all the national parks and wonders in America. I also need to support this EPIC adventure financially, which means I need to be able to work remotely.

Luckily, the value I offer as a Heart Value expert, speaker and author can roll with me, anywhere. The simple creature comforts of a mobile bed, kitchen and office free my mind and fuel my body to focus on the adventure in front of me instead of worrying about the implications of "making do" because I am concerned about the impact of my choices on others.

My desire to see the country—combined with my awareness of my own habits, nourishment requirements and need for a creative workspace—reinforced the appeal of mobile living. As I began to process my envisioning phase, I tried to imagine if I could accomplish all I wanted while navigating planes, trains and automobiles. My intuitive answer was, "No way."

Once you are *aware* of your key considerations, factors and priorities, let your imagination run wild! If you can dream it and see it, it's possible.

With clear awareness of my motivating factors, I felt that a recreational vehicle, van or kitted-out truck was my best vehicle option. From there, I did some research. I imagined myself driving, parking and living out of each one.

I paid close attention to how that visualization experience made me feel. RVs lacked character and felt big and obtrusive to me. While trucks can be super cool and have lots of character, they do not allow free movement from the driver's seat to the living quarters. Vans had the right balance of inconspicuousness, accessibility and decent gas mileage, to boot.

With the van base model as my foundational vision, my imagination went wild. Then I had to face any fears that prevented me from envisioning my ideal experience.

Of course, I had to confront a few major ones. First, I couldn't help but wonder, is this the right time to do this? Followed by, am I too old for this? Sleeping out of a van and bouncing around like I'm in my twenties? I dealt with my age-related fear very pragmatically. There's never a right time for anything, so *if not now, when*? Certainly, traveling in a van wasn't going to be more attractive in my fifties, lol.

I squashed my concern with the realization that I had the ability to stay in a hotel or rent an Airbnb if I needed a break from vanlife. Again, I could envision my EPIC adventure the way it best supported me and my needs, based on my Heart Value rules.

Second, I wondered: Am I prepared to do this alone? Luckily, I realized that I'll never be alone unless I want to be. I am blessed with two wonderful German shepherd sidekicks, Cali and Trooper, who already go everywhere with me. Cali and Trooper think they're human and they love road trips, so that's an easy win for us all.

In addition, as soon as I became more vocal about my vision and intent, I couldn't believe the positive, engaged reactions I received from friends and family.

One of my friends, Jean, flew out to Idaho to attend a vanlife festival with me, and we took over a week traveling back east before I dropped her off in Nashville to fly home.

MARY TESS ROONEY

I have many other offers to keep me company, and I suspect these folks are all intrigued enough to accompany me if I don't want to experience a particular destination alone.

I was glad I took the time to self-reflect using awareness, imagination and recognition of my fears to crystallize what I envisioned for my EPIC adventure. This step was the basis for plans I then put into place to make my vanlife dream a reality.

If you are wondering where to start, *envision* a life where your Heart Value is appreciated in ways that matter most to you. What does that environment look and feel like? What emotions surface as you stand in that world? Who is cheering you on and reflecting your extreme value back to you? What joyful activities are you incorporating to fuel your soul? Are you able to prioritize your health and fulfillment as part of your worldly obligations?

I know some people think vision boards are for woo-woo spirit junkies, but there's research to support the effectiveness of envisioning and mapping out your goals and, most importantly, your feelings associated with attaining those goals. We can look to Olympic athletes for evidence of how and why a consistent practice of visualization works.

Peak Performance Sports posted an article by Patrick Cohn titled "How Olympians Use Mental Imagery to Improve Success."[13] In it, Cohn states that, for Olympians, "Countless research studies have indicated that visualization can improve performance as much as 45 percent! The more repetitions you perform, the better you become at a task."

A 2016 *Washington Post* article by Rick Maese, "For Olympians, seeing (in their minds) is believing (it can happen),"[14] featured Guang Yue, an exercise physiologist at the Cleveland Clinic Foundation. Yue conducted a study in which volunteers *imagined* "flexing their biceps as hard as possible. After a few weeks of simply visualizing weight training, the subjects showed a 13.5 percent increase in strength."

The bottom line is, visualization has an impact, which is why most professional athletes enlist the help of sports psychologists to hone their minds and envision their desired outcomes. Vision boards, and the use of consistent visualization, are becoming more popular.

During one of my yoga retreats, I was asked to create a vision board. I enjoyed flipping through magazines, cutting out images and words that deeply resonated with me and pasting my visual cues into an artistic collage. It was fun and eye-opening to see what spoke to me. The pictures and words revolved around the great outdoors, hiking, skiing, fitness, health, organic farming, exploration, confidence, speaking up, spirituality, love, family, romance, nature and other interests.

As is true with investing in your Value Vault, the act of visualizing, reflecting and documenting what's most important to you creates an energetic shift toward the life you desire. The reflection on your Heart Value, combined with clarity around how you want to feel in the future, puts you in the best position to succeed.

Years later, I still pull out my vision portfolio to remind myself of key feelings, dreams and phrases. Yes, mine is a portfolio versus a board because I'm an explorer at heart and I wanted it to be mobile, like me (haha). My friend Bella uses an app on her phone that allows her to make a collage of her desired vision from digital images.

I currently have eight pages of images, dreams and phrases that keep me centered as I direct my path. Some of my visions have already come true. Some are still manifesting. And a few others, that I pasted in for a desired feeling, have taken shape in unexpected ways.

For example, one of the images I included is of a studio-quality microphone. Picture the big silver boom mics that radio or podcast hosts might use. I recall pasting this image into my portfolio to symbolize speaking up, using my voice and confidently sharing my message. It represented feeling heard and connecting with people that resonated with my Heart Value.

I had already learned the difference between validation and appreciation of my value,

MARY TESS ROONEY

and I knew I had to voice my value to Activate Appreciation. Fast-forward several years, and I now own a big, black studio-quality microphone that I use for my True Stride podcast. I love podcasting and sharing my message via that platform, but the idea was not on my radar, at all, when I pasted that image into my portfolio.

As *you* think about your long- and short-term feeling state, be sure to include all aspects of your life as you map your vision. Crystallize how you want to feel in and about your relationships, health, career, home, finances, hobbies, travel, spirituality, education and community. Once you envision it, you'll then plan and prepare for your adventure.

PLAN

When in corporate life, I used to write strategic plans to move the organization and thousands of employees in one direction. A strategic plan provides a public commitment of mission, vision and values. It outlines goals and action plans needed to achieve desired results.

A company's strategic plan takes its strengths, weaknesses, areas of opportunity and tactical accountability into account to ensure adoption and success. Planning allows for steady and consistent growth over time. It leaves room to integrate new opportunities and manage challenges. At an individual level, you have the opportunity to leverage your strengths and opportunities to set your plan up for success too. In a 2019 Mindvalley blog, "5 Examples of Life Goals to Motivate You to Set One Today,"[15] Irina Yugay writes: "Studies show that knowing and using our inner strengths can increase our confidence (Crabtree 2002), boost our engagement (Sorensen, 2014), and even promote feelings of good health and life satisfaction (Proyer et al., 2013)."

The planning process establishes a clear direction for where you want to go, today, tomorrow and over the next five years. Your Heart Value reflections, combined with clarity about how you want to feel in the future, puts you in the best position to succeed.

Your plan is a living document that will change over time. Review, update and celebrate the plan often to stay accountable and on track to achieve your goals and objectives.

Reverse engineer your short-term checkpoints to reach your long-term feeling finish line. Define clear priorities along with attainable actions to set yourself up for success. Flags and checkpoints serve as short-term milestones that allow you to track progress. Each checkpoint offers an opportunity for reflection, perspective and growth on your route.

If necessary, divide a long leg up into several shorter sections, even if you feel like it's more of a zigzag than a direct line. Create weekly checkpoints with flexibility for days off. Even the most rigorous marathon training plans account for rest days.

Some days, you need a break. You might have a last-minute conflict, or you might not have the energy, so set realistic plans. Start small and scale slowly. The key is to prepare to navigate the planned and unexpected events that will cross your path. If you anticipate resistance, adjust plans on the fly (with the big picture in mind).

There are many roadblocks that may stand in your way, but there's always a way to move forward if you show up with that intention and mindset. If it feels intimidating at first, that's normal. Once you understand what's involved, you need to start small and establish realistic plans.

The time you take to plan and prepare up front, before you take action, will save time and minimize frustration in the long run. Companies do this to make sure they are headed in the right direction, and you can too.

I love the planning phase of any adventure, because with enough time, energy, resources and effort, anything is possible. If you visualize your adventure and create clear priorities along with attainable actions, you set yourself up for success.

If you look at your life like this big adventure map, filled with twists, turns, breathtaking views, steep climbs, swampy pits, pristine prairies and some bloodsucking mosquitoes along the way, you'll see that your present and your future, or the path ahead,

MARY TESS ROONEY

are not yet designed. Hopefully you've spent enough time with your inner compass to know where you want to go and how long you anticipate it will take, but the direction and pace are entirely yours to choose.

Since we're using the EPIC adventure map theme to help you document your planning phase, here are some visual cues to help you creatively illustrate your plans and progress.

PLOT YOUR OWN *ADVENTURE MAP LEGEND*

- *Map:* A pictorial or illustrative representation of what you envision, short- and long-term. This provides a strong foundation before you put plans in motion to stride toward your best adventure. You can use a notebook, vision board or other resources on www.marytess-rooney.com to create your adventure map.

- *Feeling finish line:* Your long-term goal and desired outcome for how you want to feel in your life.

- *Route:* Your chosen direction that helps you plan a way to get from a starting point to a specific destination. Your route may identify multiple flags and checkpoints as next steps on your path.

- *Checkpoint:* A place along the route that incorporates accountability or a measurement to ensure that you are making progress toward your feeling finish line and celebrating your accomplishments. These can be checked personally, or you can enlist support to monitor your progress with the help of an accountability partner, buddy or coach. Checkpoints ensure that you take a moment to be present, appreciate how far you've come and continue to track toward your desired outcome. Consistent weekly checkpoints are recommended as you move through your adventure. Getting lost is okay, but checkpoints also reground you when you've gotten off track. You can reorient yourself from a checkpoint to move forward once again.

- *Green flag:* A goal in your path that you want to achieve. Green flags are short-term goals that support advancement toward your long-term, feeling finish line goal.

- *Red flag:* An obstacle or an emotional trigger in your path that causes momentary reflection or redirection. Red flags signal you to pay attention before you proceed, or proceed with caution. Sometimes red flags are helpful and insightful, like an intuitive warning that a certain path is not aligned with your Heart Value. Sometimes they are old patterns that you have to break before you can move forward, such as letting go of a limiting belief or creating a boundary with an unsupportive person in your life.

- *Path:* Your route from green flag to green flag, your strategy on how to move most effectively to reach a checkpoint—or your ability to see other possible paths if a red flag occurs.

- *Inner compass:* Your source of directional insights and information— based on your energetic, emotional, physical and spiritual aware- ness—to help you navigate toward your best adventure. When you are attuned to your inner compass, you are in harmony and moving in alignment with your Heart Value. Your inner compass offers you a gut check when navigating flags and your path.

- *Fuel:* On any adventure, your body needs fuel to stay strong and focused. It also needs fuel in the form of rest to aid with recovery time.

- *Power:* Keeping your mind sharp and your lights on.

If there are experiences and feelings in your Value Vault that you hope to *not* repeat as you plan, don't lose sight of them. Similarly, be sure to add activities to your plan that awaken your heart and energize your soul.

Think about something you want to experience and figure out how you can add it to the design of your adventure map, no matter how long it takes. You have the power to direct your path and set your pace. Don't get hung up on how long it might take.

With my clear vanlife vision in place, I moved into the tactical planning phase of my adventure. I had to research and test-drive multiple vans.

Since I'm not a skilled carpenter, I investigated van conversions and builders to support my vision. I had to account for the financial considerations: the purchase, build, insurance and all the other specifics involved in my vanlife EPIC adventure.

I also collected destination ideas, weather tips and itineraries from groups and friends. I reviewed my calendar and looked for windows of opportunity to insert business and pleasure trips.

I reverse engineered my plan and documented my journey to the best of my ability. Now, I just had to start implementing.

IMPLEMENT

I am no longer a vanlife spectator. I bought a van!!

Okay, that wasn't the first item from my plan to tackle, but it's certainly the most noteworthy, related to vanlife, anyway. Implementation is about the execution of your vision. It's taking your colorful adventure map and investing the time, energy and resources every week to navigate your path and hit your desired checkpoints.

If this is a new practice, be consistent to build muscle memory. If you miss a day, that's okay, but don't miss the weekly checkpoint.

If you miss multiple weekly checkpoint goals, evaluate which red flags are getting in your way. If your delays are unavoidable, consider revising your map checkpoints to make them more realistic and attainable. Allow for life's other demands and unexpected events to flow with your progress toward your *feeling* finish line.

Set up an accountability process or a buddy system. If you have the financial means, don't be shy about investing in resources or hiring an expert to support your progress and encourage your forward momentum.

When I decided my corporate career was no longer an ideal fit for my personal goals, I had too many financial obligations to leave right away. I had to put a multi-year plan in place, but it was realistic, and I had a clear vision. I kept showing up and putting one foot in front of the other.

I'm grateful that I committed to my path years ago, because even though it took a lot of twists and turns, I'm much happier now. As a Heart Value expert, author and speaker, I found that the execution and implementation process, moving from one action item to the next, was perfect for me.

CHERISH

The C in EPIC could easily represent celebrate or change, but I mindfully selected *cherish* because I want you to cherish what surfaces for you as you implement your plan. I want you to cherish your position of power to celebrate, choose and change as you see fit. This is your EPIC adventure, after all.

Cherish every ounce of progress you make as you envision, plan and implement your dreams. Honoring your headway—the good, the bad and the complicated—provides renewed energy and assurance that you are accruing value as you rhythmically move forward.

Every adventure will encounter a period of resistance, but once you realize your True Stride, an emotional satisfaction tends to surface. On a run, after my ten-minute resistance milestone, I go into a euphoric, meditative full-body trance. Everything just feels lighter and more fluid.

When I hit my True Stride, in running and in life, I feel invincible. I am fully attuned to my entire being, in a groove and deeply rooted in what matters. When I follow my heart, stay true to myself and connect with those who energize and appreciate me, quirks and all, I intuitively set my pace, appreciate my strength and align with my chosen path.

When you take focused moments to *cherish* your evolution, despite earlier resistance, you reap the benefits of feeling strong, empowered and energized. And the momentum generated in one area of your life will energize you in other areas of your life, too. You deserve to be aligned with your True Stride and feel that euphoric state throughout your life, so cherish all of it!

If you are not hitting your True Stride for one reason or another, it's okay. Take a deep breath and, instead of judging yourself, cherish your ability to reevaluate. Are you being impacted by roadblocks or factors outside of your control? Did your plans not work out the way you intended, leaving you with questions or doubts?

Before the COVID-19 pandemic created travel restrictions, I started to implement plans for a cross-country summer road trip. Obviously, I had to postpone that plan for safety and health reasons. While the delay affected my ability to hit the road, it offered other opportunities to gear up and get ready for when we are free to roam again.

I accepted the reality of the situation and cherished my ability to create a new EPIC adventure at home during quarantine. I can honestly say that this book would not be what it is without my ability to cherish my power to change, choose and celebrate as necessary.

Life is in a constant state of motion, so external factors, doubts and questions naturally occur in business and in life. The key is to remember that you have the freedom to choose again and change your direction at any point.

With each step—planned or unplanned—recognize how far you've come. Constantly visualize your next checkpoint marker or target before you achieve it, and then invest in your Value Vault and voice your value as you achieve checkpoints on your map. Acknowledge and cherish small wins at each milestone.

You made your value a priority by envisioning, planning and implementing your best adventure. Now you get to cherish your forward movement and gain momentum. And remember, you don't have to collect all the checkpoint markers!

CHECKPOINT: DEVELOP YOUR EPIC ADVENTURE

As you reflect, notice your emotional responses. Each heart-centered feeling that surfaces provides clues that will influence your choices and inform your actions.

Instrumental Insights

~ Your EPIC adventure is an individualized journey in which you envision, plan, implement and cherish your best life. The four-step process, combined with your strategy, smarts, stamina and strength, empowers you to:

~ *Envision* where you want to go in life, based on how you want to feel.

~ *Plan* your route and map paths with a series of flags and checkpoints to help you advance toward your feeling finish line.

~ *Implement* that plan using time, energy and resources to support your advancement each step of the way.

~ *Cherish* your progress, momentum and ability to *choose again* if the road you are traveling no longer resonates with you.

WISE WALK REFLECTION

Journal without judgment and process these Wise Walk questions to gain awareness.

1. As you envision your *long- and short-term feeling states*, how do you want to *feel* in and about your relationships, health, career, home, finances, hobbies, travel, spirituality, education and community?

2. What is one choice you can make that creates an energetic and emotional connection to your experiences, people and activities?

3. If you are not energetically or emotionally aligned with something, what action will you take to release yourself from that experience, person, place or thing?

FEEL-CHOOSE-ACT AMPLIFIER

Observe an area in your life that you'd like to address and apply this feel, choose and act amplifier. Jump right in, or read the following examples to get your Feel-Choose-Act juices flowing.

Feel	Choose	Act

Feel > Choose > Act

Feel	Choose	Act
I am excited and energized to explore national parks and visit friends near and far.	I chose vanlife to support my health-conscious eating choices and career goals while enjoying adventures on the road.	I have a list of national parks I want to visit, and I'll act on it.

Affirmation

My Heart Value is a priority and I live my EPIC adventure every day.

Tip:

Your EPIC adventure is full of possibilities. The first step is designing where you want to go and how you want to feel when you get there.

Notes:

Get Your Stride On

Every living thing deserves to vibrate at a
higher frequency and feel appreciated in
ways that matter.

MARY TESS ROONEY

Endnotes

13   Patrick Cohn, "How Olympians Use Mental Imagery to Improve Success," PeakSports.com, last accessed June 15, 2021, https://www.peaksports.com/sports-psychology-blog/how-olympians-use-mental-imagery-to-improve-success/.

14   Rick Maese, "For Olympians, seeing (in their minds) is believing (it can happen)," WashingtonPost.com, July 28, 2016, https://www.washingtonpost.com/sports/olympics/for-olympians-seeing-in-their-minds-is-believing-it-can-happen/2016/07/28/6966709c-532e-11e6-bbf5-957ad17b4385_story.html.

15   Irina Yugay, "5 Examples of Life Goals to Motivate You to Set One Today," Mindvalley.com, January 16, 2019, https://blog.mindvalley.com/life-goals/.

CHAPTER 9

GET YOUR STRIDE ON: ACTIVATE APPRECIATION

Visibility is one of the best ways to attract opportunities that align with what you stand for and love about your gifts and abilities. The value you offer and the imprint you leave are far too important to be forgotten.

As I drove home from an adventure-filled weekend with my exhausted nieces and nephews, I could feel our energy drain and happy dispositions begin to fade. What started off as normal brother-sister teasing began to take a merciless turn.

We were at a slow crawl on the New Jersey Turnpike in my cousin's Suburban when the words "You. Will. Be. In. Big. Trouble." flew out of my mouth. I flinched and held my breath as I waited to see my nieces' and nephews' response. They looked shocked, but remained silent. Everyone's hands rested quietly in their own laps. Whew, no response.

I took a breath and stared wide-eyed at the sea of red taillights ahead of me. Then a wave of anxiety rushed over me as I realized I had no idea what "You will be in big trouble" meant. I didn't have children of my own. I had overheard that threat from other adults as something they'd say before doling out consequences, but my words were baseless. I didn't have any idea what I'd do if they tested me.

Yikes, what if they test me?! My white-knuckled hands clenched the steering wheel as I considered my options. *Will I pull over on the side of the road and…nah, we're barely moving as it is…. Dear Lord, what do other people mean when they say it?*

I turned on some music so I could distract the kids while I pretended to be calm, but I was freaking out inside. I called my mom.

"Mom," I whispered in the phone so the kiddos couldn't hear me. "The kids were getting rowdy in the back of the car with some physical contact beginning to escalate, and I yelled out that Big Trouble warning, but I have no idea what that means. Help! What if they test me?"

"Well, did you say it with authority?" Mom asked.

"Yes," I replied.

"Then that's all that matters."

I share this story because, if I were sitting beside you as you read this book, that is what I'd say to you *if* you don't apply all the clarity, tangible examples and guidance that you've created for yourself. Yes, you will be in big trouble.

Clearly, I don't know what big trouble means for you, but you deserve to feel seen, understood and appreciated for your Heart Value—so make that, along with fun, your priority.

Now that you've designed your EPIC adventure, it's time to *get your stride on!* First, acknowledge yourself for all of the self-reflective, strategic and tactical exercises you've successfully completed in the previous chapters! Woo-hoo!

Learning to trust your inner compass is commendable. Prioritizing your value and appreciation sweet spot over external expectations and pressures is brave. The awareness, clarity and confidence you've gained are accomplishments that will fuel your momentum with each step you take.

When I became self-employed, I suffered from random bouts of doubt and anxiety. My ego loved to hiss, "Get a *real* job that offers a stable paycheck, healthcare and benefits." On the days I silenced my ego, I had well-intentioned friends or family members express similar sentiments. ("Ruh-roh," as Scooby-Doo would say.)

Thankfully, all my internal work to invest in my Value Vault, trust my inner compass and design my EPIC adventure paid off. My desire to surround myself with Heart Value relationships and have this value conversation with *you* suppressed those nagging voices of uncertainty and doubt.

The self-work leading up to this chapter gave me the courage, chops and fortitude to lovingly check my ego and tell my well-meaning family, "Thanks, I appreciate your concern, but I'm excited about my new path."

In hindsight, I get that no one was necessarily trying to change my mind. They simply wanted me to reassure them that I had thought this decision through.

As with any new activity or muscle development, my transition seemed challenging, clunky and slow at first. It took time for my family members, and my ego, to come around to this new way of being. It was a new path for all of us, but I knew that once I hit my True Stride, everything would feel more fluid.

The key, for me, was to determine what support I needed to get my stride on. I knew that my plans, both present and future, included symbiotic, energetic and emotional connections that fueled me and brought more skip to my step.

With a focus on what I would *gain* by creating more room in my life, I said bye-bye to my corporate attire, doubts and people who were uncomfortable with the changes I had made. My award-smashing party was a small part of that purging exercise.

With each release of the old, my odds for success and ability to get my stride on increased substantially. This support lens spanned all influences in my life including people, places and possessions. And yes, I felt lighter and happier after I released what didn't align with my vision.

As I made space for the life I wanted, I realized that while doubt is natural, it's super heavy. There's a metaphorical and sometimes literal weight to thoughts, things and old habits that impede forward movement. For example, if I wanted to move with greater ease, I needed to lighten my load, so to speak. This meant purging old, formal corporate writing habits and belief systems that aren't necessary in my current adventure.

As you look at your EPIC adventure map, ask yourself: Are certain areas in your life slowing you down or derailing your progress? What past choices, relationships, patterns or possessions no longer serve you? Who connects with your Heart Value and supports your chosen path? Who makes a deposit in your Value Vault, and who makes withdrawals without replenishing your emotional and energetic well-being?

SHIFT FROM TRANSACTIONAL TO TRANSFORMATIONAL

Rhonda, an accomplished author, speaker and educator who empowered individuals and teams to unleash their creativity, had a pivotal Heart Value awakening and True Stride turning point.

For over five years, she was called to share her creativity and innovation speech across the globe with others. Her presentation and message were unique, motivational and polished, but she could barely make ends meet. In her forties, she was single and without savings or a retirement plan.

Rhonda's strong self-belief drove her to keep moving forward, even when she had to take a shared car service to the airport for her next contracted speaking gig because she couldn't afford to ride solo.

She had been pitching her content, workshops and keynote speech to the technology industry. She believed that tech-savvy audiences would benefit most from her message about inspired creativity and innovation without limits. The less-than-enthusiastic feedback and lack of referrals suggested otherwise. She landed minimal paid gigs and every day seemed like a slog.

Rhonda, a fierce and talented speaker, knew her value with this audience was invisible. The tech industry did not connect with her Heart Value, and it was time for a change.

Before she raised the white flag on her speaking career or explored ways to tweak her content, she decided to test her intellectual property on a completely different audience. Intuitively, she knew that her ego needed a boost, so she scanned her social media connections to find a friendly face in any type of corporate role. Her high school buddy, Brad, jumped out immediately. She hadn't spoken to him in decades, but he held a marketing role at a tire company and Rhonda thought, "I've got nothing to lose."

By chance, Brad was planning to host a marketing department staff meeting and booked Rhonda after their initial call. Her presentation was a massive success.

Rhonda immediately noticed a dramatic difference in how her material and message, the very same content she had offered to the tech-savvy teams, resonated with Brad's team. The energy, vibration and frequency of that meeting gave her goosebumps. She immediately felt a Heart Value connection and began to wonder why she had spent so much time trying to feel visible and appreciated by the technology industry.

Her leap of faith, reaching out to an old high school classmate, reinforced that it was possible to *activate the appreciation* she deserved. Rhonda was proactive in discovering her audience, and they felt lucky to have found her. She was grateful that her self-belief had compelled her to reach out to Brad, instead of raising the white flag, and she felt invigorated when she saw that her Heart Value was finally seen and appreciated. Her connection with Brad resulted in three credible referrals!

The momentum Rhonda gained from that one high school connection set her career on fire. The growth trajectory seemed overwhelming at first, but the demand and flow of referrals allowed her to increase her speaking fees and rightfully enjoy some well-earned financial freedom.

She even received recognition from other renowned speakers, like Brené Brown. What's interesting is, her speech and content were the same. The only thing she changed was the audience, and her intention to attract more of that ideal audience. That decision moved her from broke, unfulfilled and deflated to prosperous, happy and energized.

Thankfully, Rhonda *trusted her inner compass* and didn't give up on her ability to impact lives. Once she overcame her disappointment and subsequent focus on the disconnect with her audience, her renewed mindset sent a signal to the universe to find attendees that resonated with her message and vibration. And guess what, they appeared.

As you think about the individuals or experiences you want to attract in your life, are you conscious of your thoughts and intentions?

Jack Canfield, the cocreator of *Chicken Soup for the Soul* and the author of multiple bestsellers, empowers individuals to use the Law of Attraction to create the lives and results they want. His book *The Success Principles*[16] reminds us that since "you'll attract into your life whatever you give your energy, focus and attention to—wanted or un-wanted—you must become more deliberate about what you think and feel." That is the essence of the Law of Attraction. The frequency of your thoughts and energy are felt, and that vibration will be matched and returned to you, energetically speaking. Positive vibrations attract positive people, places and things, while negative feelings bring about more negative experiences. As Richard Bach wrote, "Like attracts like."[17]

Obviously, remaining positive in our thoughts and feelings can be hard some days, but time and again we realize benefits from radiating positive energy and allowing the universe to respond in kind. That's why the checkpoint affirmations at the end of each chapter are so important. Since the universe will match the energy you emit, a positive affirmation repeated out loud or handwritten several times vibrates that desired feeling state. Affirmations reinforce a positive attitude toward what you seek. Reciting the affirmation and "acting as if" will help you channel positive thoughts so you can align with that vibration and feeling state.

Jack Canfield describes this send-and-receive exchange of frequencies this way: "You are like a radio station that is broadcasting on a specific frequency.... If you want more abundance and prosperity in your life, you have to tune the frequency of your thoughts and feelings to ones of abundance and prosperity."[18]

I'm always amazed at positive or negative shifts that occur depending on my state of mind, the thoughts I hold in my heart or the people in my life. That's why I purposefully make choices and take action to vibrate love, joy, laughter, fun and appreciation. The more the universe matches me with high vibrational

Transformational relationships offer a mutual exchange of Heart Value that feels energizing, fulfilling and rewarding.

Notes:

experiences, the more I realize my True Stride. As you get your stride on, a little momentum will help you attract more of what you seek, too.

As you assess the relationships in your life, ask yourself: Which of them feel transformational, versus transactional? A transformational relationship invites you to flourish, evolve and expand into the human you are or long to be. Transformational relationships make a positive impact and impression on us, whether the other people involved know it or not. Heart Value relationships are transformational because they are based on mutual appreciation and an exchange of energies and emotion that feels fulfilling.

On the flip side, in a transactional relationship, there's just an exchange or interaction between people, with no energetic or emotional connection or lasting imprint to inspire you. A transactional relationship might include validation for a job well done or an acknowledgment of services, but no emotion is transferred. Transactional exchanges are a necessary part of life and serve a purpose, but are there transactional relationships you are ready to release with the intention of upgrading to more Heart Value relationships?

HEART VALUE AS CURRENCY

I like to think of Heart Value as a currency that, when invested with the right people, is a natural give-and-take that grows exponentially. This type of exchange is free-flowing and frictionless, so you move with ease.

MARY TESS ROONEY

Remember my boss, Sachiel, who appreciated my Heart Value and acted as my PR agent? I thrived both professionally and personally under his leadership. We were real with each other and genuinely wanted the best for one another.

Don't change yourself to please someone else. If you sense a change is necessary to find your groove, consider changing your surroundings, whether that includes your audience, environment or material possessions.

Heart Value relationships energize your soul, creativity, happiness, health, wealth and prosperity. Someone wise once said, "People come into your life for a season, a reason or a lifetime." If you are serious about getting your stride on, you need to take a close look at the people, places and things that energize or deplete you.

What you focus on becomes your reality, so choose to focus on the energized feeling and high you receive when you share your Heart Value. By *proactively* using your inner compass and Value Vault to Activate Appreciation, you will attract more of what you actually want and less of what you don't.

Your stride is how you carry yourself with any forward movement. I say "forward" because with every interaction, observation, experience and event, we gain value. Before we take each intentional step, we have the ability to pause, slow down, speed up or change direction. Each person's stride, walk, gait, pace and movement are unique, and only you know what tempo or movement is required at each moment.

As we remain present to our surroundings and state of mind, we can recalibrate our stride and how we feel. Ultimately, we decide who we want to be.

DIFFUSE DISTRACTION BOMBS

Too often, a chunk of our day or hour is allocated to what I call "Distraction Bombs." Distraction Bombs are unexpected demands, problems, events or dramatic conversations that take us away from our focus and daily objectives. Forgotten chores that pop up, illnesses, fights with loved ones, work challenges and transportation issues are several examples of Distraction Bombs.

I coined the phrase after experiencing too many detours that interfered with my main priorities. Sadly, Distraction Bombs are usually emotionally charged and deplete us of our precious energy.

For example, if I had to miss a family dinner or reschedule a fun outing with friends due to a last-minute work crisis, I was so bummed. Yes, that was my job at the time, but interference with other key priorities in our lives should be the exception, not the norm.

In dealing with Distraction Bombs, I realized that they had a negative impact on my ability to focus and get my stride on. When obstacles arise, getting frustrated is an understandable reaction. But diversions are an everyday occurrence, so how can you continue to get your stride on in the face of adversity?

Personally, I've found that the best way to diffuse a metaphorical bomb is to either *prevent* or *embrace* it. *Prevention* is the art of managing your calendar to anticipate the unexpected in such a way that it does not take you off course.

Raphael, a successful music executive, only commits to one nonnegotiable objective per day. Sure, he may accomplish twenty-plus goals in a day, but his daily *commitment to just one* offers him the flexibility to cope with a Distraction Bomb without losing sight of his number one priority. He is crystal clear on what he will accomplish by the end of the day, whether the goal is personal or professional. Since his team, loved ones and customers all understand his philosophy, he sets himself up for success because everyone understands the expectations. In addition, he prevents potential emotional stress caused by overcommitment.

As you probably know by now, I am an overachiever by nature. I used to pride myself on managing the unexpected gracefully, amidst a full calendar, until I realized the costs and that Raphael's approach was healthier in many ways.

MARY TESS ROONEY

Since I know that overscheduling and prioritizing others' needs above my own has negative ramifications, I decided to incorporate a variation of Raphael's process. I commit to three nonnegotiable goals per day, versus his one.

Exercise and meditation are important daily activities for me, so my priorities might include nourishment for my well-being and a wild card that is usually relationship-, purpose- or contribution-related. Like Raphael, I may accomplish more than three goals per day, but this narrow focus and up-front expectation creates space to be realistic in case a Distraction Bomb surfaces.

The other way to diffuse a Distraction Bomb is to *embrace* it. Have you ever looked closely at how water rolls off of a duck's back? It's a non-event for the duck. The water promptly beads on the surface of its feathers and trickles down without any effort or concern on the duck's part.

That's the visual I use to embrace a Distraction Bomb. If I don't allow it to take hold of my focus, I am free to redirect my attention to things that truly matter to me and the rest will roll off my back.

When you plan your day the night before, chart a clear path toward your nonnegotiable checkpoints. Mentally orchestrate the seamless execution of your to-dos, and remember to create space to embrace or prevent any Distraction Bombs you may encounter. And when a Distraction Bomb surfaces, don't be afraid to follow your resonant choice and say no to rerouting your day so you can get your groove back.

Distraction Bombs are unexpected demands, problems, events or dramatic conversations that take you away from your focus and daily objectives.

Notes:

A **resonant choice** is one that aligns with the perspective that feels right to *you*.

Notes:

YOUR TRUE STRIDE RESONANT CHOICE

In coaching, we talk a lot about uncovering and following your *resonant choice*. A resonant choice is one that aligns with the perspective that feels right to *you*. The real you, no one else. The *real you*, meaning your natural, magnificent and amazing self—who you were born to be, unveiled and out of the shadows.

Yes, this means releasing the idea of who you *should* be and allowing who you long to be to surface, quirks, freak flag and all!

Admittedly, this isn't always easy. We humans are creatures of habit. Change is hard, but you already mapped out your EPIC adventure, so stay strong and don't lose sight of it. Let your resonant choices empower the real you to get your stride on and activate the appreciation you deserve. Each resonant step feeds your energy, which invigorates momentum over time. Momentum fosters acceleration, grace and ease.

I have trained for four marathons and successfully completed two. On two attempts, I never made it to the starting line, let alone the finish line.

The first failed attempt at running the 26.2-mile race was due to poor planning. I didn't honor the suggested twenty-week training program and took a lot of liberties with the weekly mile recommendations and ramp-up period. Plus, I tried to keep up with my social activities and NYC nightlife as usual, which meant staying out late with friends and then trying to ramp up my miles. Yeah, that approach was unsustainable and didn't really work for me.

MARY TESS ROONEY

The second attempt was because I overprepared, got too cocky and thought my body was indestructible. With two weeks remaining before marathon day, I was in superb shape and I had successfully logged my long run of twenty miles. It was a breathtaking run from San Francisco's Golden Gate Bridge to Tiburon, and I barely broke a sweat. I thought I had this marathon in the bag. I had already learned the lesson of saying no to the distraction of late nights when training, so I was disciplined on the nightlife front, but this time I had a different lesson to learn.

I was feeling great, and my idea of a taper (aka, giving my body a rest before marathon day) included playing coed soccer in a recreational league. The playing wasn't necessarily the problem, although friends warned me that it was an unnecessary risk, but deciding to slide-tackle a dude for the ball promptly sidelined me with an injury that required surgery. Bad decision, major Distraction Bomb and ouch!

Marathon training, like life, is much more than a physical feat. Training and preparing for a 26.2-mile race are as much about what you say *yes* to as what you say *no* to.

You absolutely have to complete the physical requirements by logging the miles, and you have to mindfully manage all other activities, commitments and support in your life to accomplish that feat.

My next two marathon training programs were successful. I applied everything I learned from the prior two attempts and, in 2004 and 2006, I finished the New York City Marathon.

I literally got my stride on! My success in those two events can be attributed to my ability to diffuse Distraction Bombs and follow my resonant choices. I also found running buddies and recruited fans, because that makes the adventure more fun, meaningful and memorable.

What's even cooler is that on the actual race days, I had a narrow focus of three priorities: Stop and say hello to all loved ones who came out to cheer me on; run for the experience, not time; and cross the finish line. I accomplished all three for both marathons and loved the feeling of success on my own terms.

HEART VALUE ZONE

Most companies invest in a customer relationship management (CRM) solution to document their customers' goals, activities, transactions and communications as a means to strengthen relationships, uncover opportunities, manage accountability and ultimately increase revenue. When used consistently and effectively, CRMs allow professionals and support teams to collaborate and meet company and client expectations.

I've been around CRMs my entire career. I've used them to have more productive conversations with my manager and clients. Or I've held oversight positions to train, communicate best practices and illustrate effective CRM use. The most successful CRM users have two simple goals in mind: nurture customer relationships and achieve revenue expectations.

And yes, happy customers who feel heard, valued and supported generally buy more, so that naturally translates to increased revenues. Savvy CRM users understand how to use the reports to look for trends and proactively identify opportunities to make more money. They evaluate all business activities against the simple question: "Will this activity lead to satisfied customers and additional revenue?" And they are brave enough to eliminate an activity if the answer is no.

One exceptional sales executive, Gabriel, exemplified this approach. Gabriel pulled reports and masterfully made connections between his revenue highs and the correlated sales activity. Responsible for millions in revenue, he discovered that his sales teams needed to conduct one hundred client-facing appointments a week to achieve their sales goals in eight weeks.

This meant that each sales professional needed at least ten quality customer appointments a week. On the surface, the targets seemed reasonable—until Gabriel realized those numbers didn't account for time off or time allocated for internal company meetings.

Ironically, as Gabriel assessed the factors that prevented the need for ten appointments a week, he discovered that he and his management team were the biggest offenders.

They would tout client-facing time as the biggest priority, but they inadvertently limited client appointments by offering trainings or mandatory all-staff meetings in the middle of the day or during prime selling times. Add in a company holiday, vacation or sick leave, and the overall goal of one hundred appointments a week seemed unattainable. Fewer appointments consistently translated to a revenue loss eight weeks later.

To Gabriel's credit, he understood what he and his sales force would *gain* by releasing activities that didn't serve the main objective of nurturing the client relationship to make more money. And he was brave enough to challenge his management team to embrace this strategy.

His team creatively drove client-facing interactions before and after times when people tended to be out on vacation and offered sales contests and incentives to increase activity around holiday months and school breaks. Because of this, Gabriel enjoyed over sixty consecutive months of hitting his budget and receiving exceptional employee satisfaction scores.

Time is our most precious resource. What we do or don't do on any given day will impact how we feel today and may affect our goal attainment several weeks from now.

I've upgraded from CRM use to a Heart Value Zone (HVZ, lol) process, so I can evaluate what activities, relationships and information support my Heart Value and highest joy frequency. The HVZ questions I use are available to you in Bonus Adventure 2 at the back of this book.

My EPIC adventure map is my visual reference that reminds me of the checkpoints

I want to attain. I don't allow my calendar to fill with meetings without checking those activities against the simple question: "Will this elevate my joy frequency?"

Sharing my Heart Value brings me, and those who appreciate me, tremendous joy. That's the feeling and frequency I want to radiate today and many weeks from now.

THE PROACTIVE POWER OF A PUBLICIST

In the world of public relations, PR agents don't wait for influencers or members of the press to come to them. They proactively evaluate *who aligns with* or *has an interest* in what they have to say or offer.

If you want to get your stride on and gain momentum, it's best to take a proactive approach to determining *who aligns with* or *has an interest* in the value you offer. Follow Rhonda's example and scroll through your phone, Facebook, LinkedIn, Instagram, Pinterest, Twitter and other contacts to explore which relationships energize or emotionally connect with you. Keep an open mind, but trust your inner compass and follow your instincts.

Behind every successful business, leader or speaker, there's a dedicated PR agent, publicist or communications professional managing their value messages, generating media coverage and seeking opportunities to raise their reputation. A publicist gets paid to do this for other people. Ironically, it's commonly accepted among PR firms and communication professionals alike that while they are diligent at doing this for others, they are the worst at doing it for themselves. I too fell into this bad habit.

For years, I was a communications professional who prided myself on raising the profiles of my executives and widely sharing their successes and business wins. I thought, "If my leaders and company look good, then I look good." What I learned is that it's nearly impossible to Activate Appreciation for your value if you choose to remain in the shadows.

MARY TESS ROONEY

What makes publicists tick? Being armed with amazing stories and case studies to demonstrate value and impact. You are already the most qualified expert on *you*, your stories and impact, so why not act as your own PR agent, daily? Be proactive in looking for opportunities to get your Heart Value out there using your *contacts, calendar* and *communications channels.*

For *contacts*, prioritize your top targets and your low-hanging fruit. Who can help your value be heard, understood and appreciated? What tangible examples illustrate and reinforce your Heart Value?

People are attracted to smart investments and shiny objects, so make bold choices to stand out. Visibility is one of the best ways to attract opportunities that align with what you stand for and love about your gifts and abilities. The value you offer and the imprint you leave are far too important to be forgotten.

Use your *calendar* to look forward and be proactive versus reactive. Create an editorial calendar and look for opportunities get on editors' radar to tell your story. Are there speaking or seasonal opportunities that reinforce your value? Are there events or groups who are ready to listen to your story? When will you pitch your Heart Value and engage support to increase awareness of *you*?

With your impressive Value Vault in hand, use your calendar to schedule time with key influencers and ask them to advocate for your contributions and impact. Commit to proactively voicing your value once a day, or at minimum once a week, to start.

Evaluate your *communications channels*, social media presence and technology platforms to increase your share of voice. Creating a broader awareness of your unique value will empower influencers and champions to position you to receive opportunities that align with your Heart Value and help you feel appreciated in the ways that matter most.

Build a tribe of supporters who recognize your value and enlist others who would benefit from your talents. The goal is to create a stereo effect so you can build PR advocates without effort. When jobs or interests that align with your value and passions become available, your network will notify you because your Heart Value is fresh in their minds.

Let the vibration and volume of your voice penetrate your *contacts*, *calendar* and *communications channels* to create a cascade effect, with or without your presence.

CHECKPOINT: GET YOUR STRIDE ON!

As you reflect, notice your emotional responses. Each heart-centered feeling that surfaces provides clues that will influence your choices and inform your actions.

Instrumental Insights

- Heart Value relationships energize your soul, creativity, happiness, health, wealth and prosperity.

- What you do or don't do on any given day will impact how you feel today and may affect your goal attainment several weeks from now.

- You are already the most qualified expert on *you*, your stories and impact, so why not act as your own PR agent, daily? Look for proactive opportunities to get your Heart Value seen and heard using your *contacts*, *calendar* and *communications channels*.

- For *contacts*, prioritize your top targets and your low-hanging fruit. Who can help your value be heard, understood and appreciated? What tangible examples illustrate and reinforce your Heart Value?

- People are attracted to smart investments and shiny objects, so make bold choices to stand out.

MARY TESS ROONEY

- With your impressive Value Vault in hand, use your *calendar* to look forward and be proactive. Are there speaking or seasonal opportunities that reinforce your value? Are there events or groups who are ready to listen to your story? When will you pitch your Heart Value and engage support to increase awareness of *you*?

- Commit to proactively voicing your value once a day, or at minimum once a week, to start. Use your calendar to schedule time with key influencers and ask them to advocate for your contributions and impact.

- Evaluate your *communications channels*, social media presence and technology platforms to increase your share of voice. Create a broader awareness of your unique value to receive opportunities that align with your Heart Value and help you feel appreciated in the ways that matter most.

- Build a tribe of supporters to create a stereo effect so you can activate your PR agents without effort.

WISE WALK REFLECTION

Journal without judgment and process these Wise Walk questions to gain awareness.

1. As you consider using your *contacts*, *calendar* and *communications channels* to proactively promote your worth, what emotions and feelings surface? If you feel resistance, what's that about?

2. As you evaluate your contacts, calendar and communications

channels, ask yourself: Which options energize you and will set you up for success? If you feel overwhelmed by the choices you want to make to proactively promote your worth, do you have someone—a PR agent or accountability partner—who is willing to support and mentor you as you raise your Heart Value vibration?

3. Select one action you will take this week to Activate Appreciation. How does that one action support your short- and long-term goals?

FEEL-CHOOSE-ACT AMPLIFIER

Observe an area in your life that you'd like to address and apply this feel, choose and act amplifier. Jump right in, or read the following examples to get your Feel-Choose-Act juices flowing.

Feel	Choose	Act

MARY TESS ROONEY

Feel	Choose	Act

Feel	Choose	Act
Rhonda wanted to feel appreciated for her Heart Value.	She believed in her message and speech, so she made a choice to keep her content the same while she explored other potential audiences.	Her action and determination resulted in her connection with a new industry that loved her content and speech exactly as they are.

Affirmation

I constantly attract Heart Value relationships that energetically and emotionally appreciate who I am and all that I offer.

Tip:

By proactively using your Value Vault, inner compass and Heart Value to Activate Appreciation, you will attract more of what you want and less of what you don't. Focus on what you want to get your stride on!

Notes:

Get Your Stride On

You deserve to feel seen, understood
and appreciated for your Heart Value—so
make that, along with fun, your priority.

Endnotes

16   Jack Canfield, *The Success Principles* (New York: HarperCollins, 2005), p. 64.

17   Richard Bach, *Illusions: The Adventures of a Reluctant Messiah* (New York: Dell Publishing Co., 1977).

18   Canfield, *The Success Principles*, p. 72.

MARY TESS ROONEY

CHAPTER 10

MY SOMETHING AND EPIC ADVENTURE

My something *included surrounding myself with individuals whose hearts crave more meaningful relationships, joy and fulfillment.*

Jade, a smart and sweet twenty-one-year-old college student, was in town visiting family when I asked her over for tea. As I gave her a hug, I could feel the weight of the world on her shoulders. Ugh, my heart hurt for her, because even without any context, I could tell her inner light felt dim.

I embraced her tighter and longer than I would in a typical hug because I wanted her to feel my energy of possibilities, love and support. Not just in that moment, but in the future she had yet to create for herself.

She fought back her tears and laughed nervously, sensing my strong energy and knowing I wasn't going to let her get away with small talk. I looked her in her eyes and said, "I see you, Jade. Tell me what's going on in that big, beautiful heart of yours." I wanted to know what she was authentically feeling as she approached graduation.

Slightly embarrassed that my embrace made her eyes well up, she pulled back and spoke from her brain, providing me with logical reasons why she was considering a career as a logistician. Hmm... I didn't even know what a logistician was, so I asked.

She admitted that she wasn't exactly sure herself, but with her business degree, it would be a good, stable job with healthcare benefits. Ouch, my heart hurt for her a little more. What concerned me wasn't what she said; it was the matter-of-fact way she said it. She sounded positively lifeless as she described the next chapter of her adventure. She was detached from her *feelings* and spoke of her *choices* as if reciting from a script someone else (very well-intentioned, I'm sure) had given her.

I had deep empathy for Jade because I've been there. In the absence of identifying our *something* and knowing what *we* want, we seek counsel from trusted advisors or loved ones to direct our path. Our family, friends and mentors know us. *Shouldn't* they know what's best for us long-term? Yuck, there's that *should* again.

Anyone who cares about you will happily share their opinions and offer advice on what your *something* should be according to made-up rules. That's great for them, but *you* are not them. The individuals *without* an agenda or skin in the game may have your best interests at heart, but *you* are the only one who can read the signs, direct your path and get your stride on, at least according to *your own* Heart Value rules.

When I graduated from college, I was Jade. I was on the hunt for money to pay the bills and live in Manhattan. My focus was to accept new "adult" responsibility, which in my mind meant prioritizing career, success and healthcare benefits. I had some fun gigs and great experiences and, before I knew it, I got swept up in my career trajectory.

MARY TESS ROONEY

My busy life required so much headspace, I forgot to lead with my heart. Unconsciously, mindlessly, I followed everyone else's adventure map and definition of success.

I unintentionally climbed the corporate ladder and reached an executive suite. Along the way, I had experiences where I felt valued and appreciated, and moments where I felt invisible, misunderstood or overlooked.

To be clear, I had a great career, and I treasure the Heart Value relationships I made along the way. I learned a ton about myself: Who I am, what lights me up and what I want.

But at some point, my inner compass was overshadowed by external expectations of what others deemed valuable. I accepted accolades when I really craved genuine appreciation. By society's standards, I had been thriving in a hustle-and-bustle world, but I realized that I was playing by made-up rules and prioritizing everyone else's adventure map over my own. The operative words there are "my own."

Thankfully, through this Heart Value awakening, I applied everything in this book to reclaim my power, reaffirm my value and activate appreciation in ways that matter most to *me*. It didn't happen overnight, but I treated my steps and missteps as I would any adventure. I methodically made strides from one trail to the next. Each path built my confidence and muscle memory. Each experience honed my ability to trust my inner compass and define my own Heart Value rules so I could realize my True Stride. I gained joy and momentum with each and every step.

Your life's adventure map is uniquely shaped by who you are, the trails you encounter, the paths you take, the experiences you have and the desires you hold in your heart. You are the expert on you, and you get to create your short- and long-term checkpoints along the way.

No two adventures are the same. No two people are the same or want the same *something* in their heart. It's your responsibility to apply everything you learned about yourself by investing in your Value Vault, designing your EPIC adventure and defining your Joy Frequency Grid—to name a few—so you can intentionally navigate your best life.

WISE WALK REFLECTIONS

My mom and I often walk on the beach together to check in and touch base. Depending on the day and our mood, we sometimes have self-reflective conversations about our past, our present and our future. We are both empaths, which means we sense energy and emotions in all *external elements*—people, places, activities and things.

Because we are attuned to the energy in and around us, walking helps to ground us in our truth and gain clarity around what—in our heart of hearts—we want as we move forward. If either one of us feels stuck or unsure, we ask each other deep questions to reveal our feeling responses and explore possibilities.

That's how Wise Walks were born. The physical movement paired, with a safe space to slow down and check our reality, formed a self-discovery muscle memory that I cherish whether I'm walking side by side with Mom or not.

As a kid, if I was struggling or in any kind of trouble, my mom would tell me to get in the car. "Let's go for a ride," she'd say. I didn't realize it at the time, but she was creating a safe space for me to confront my disconnect, speak my heart-centered truth and reveal whatever was ailing me, away from distractions and my sisters' listening ears.

Energetically and emotionally, we know, sense and feel when something is off, but you have to develop that muscle memory to read *your* signs and identify your *something*. I think of Wise Walks as an opportunity to slow down, check myself and engage my heart-center to feel, choose and act with intention.

Let me say that again: Wise Walks offer you an opportunity to slow down, check your current reality and engage your inner compass to feel, choose and act with intention.

MARY TESS ROONEY

How are you tuning into your feelings and channeling your True Stride to move forward in an optimal, connected, aligned way?

If you only take one thing from this book, find your version of a Wise Walk. Take time to reflect with physical movement or go for a drive to enjoy uninterrupted alone time. With Jade, I created a safe space for her to slow down and confront her own realizations over tea. How or where you carve out your reflective alone time is not important. The fundamental components of a Wise Walk Reflection are:

1. Alone time in a nurturing space away from demands, distractions and external pressures.

2. Courage to seek answers to your heartfelt questions. Meaningful feel, choose and act prompts will reveal your current state, surface your heart-centered reactions and advise your go-forward strategy. Walk alone, or with a trusted companion who doesn't have a personal stake in your responses and answers.

3. Nonjudgment and acceptance of what your heart wants you to know about your *something*. You may not always embrace or act on what you discover, but listen to the clues of your *something* to explore what's possible.

I've said this before, but it's worth repeating: Your heart is vital. It sustains your life, reveals who you are and encourages you to become who you were meant to be. Your feelings are central to everything you do, but from a young age we are conditioned to overthink, overanalyze and dismiss our feelings for the sake of logic or what others deem "right" for us. Thankfully, your emotional and energetic responses—yes, the good, the bad, the complicated and the ugly—are guiding you to discover your *something* and live a full experience.

If you don't know your Heart Value, you run the risk of doing what others want or expect of you. I admit that I did that in the past; sometimes going with the program seemed easier than going against the grain, which can be challenging, confusing or scary. Exploration is a critical part of self-discovery. Now that I've experienced life according to made-up rules and life according to my Heart Value rules, I'll choose my Heart Value rules every single time because my feelings matter.

It is your time to break your own mental chains, defy made-up rules and ignore limiting beliefs that hold you back from your *something*. When you learn to listen to and lead from your heart, your inner compass becomes more accurate and better equipped to direct your path. Don't waste another precious minute: Unlock your Heart Value and design your EPIC adventure to help you get your stride on.

If you've read this far and some of the reflections or checkpoints still feel unnatural to you, that's okay. We each realize our True Stride according to our own unique rhythm, flow and pace. Anything new is awkward at first—until we develop muscle memory and build our confidence.

As we discussed earlier, muscle memory becomes our unconscious response. It's a mindset, movement or pattern that becomes second nature after consistent practice. It's as if, after much repetition and refinement, we store the necessary abilities, commands and memory in our muscle tissue to call upon as needed.

Some simple examples of muscle memory are driving a vehicle or brushing your teeth. The more you practice driving, the better equipped you become to unconsciously respond to the car and your surroundings, traffic, weather challenges or winding roads.

After a consistent period of practice, energy and effort, your ingrained muscle memory triggers you to automatically put the blinker on to signal a turn or apply the right amount of pressure to the brakes to gradually come to a stop.

Your application of Wise Walk Reflections and the Feel-Choose-Act Amplifier is similar. The more you make space for these practices, the more they will become second nature to you. As with driving, at some point, your muscle memory will kick in. And the more you prioritize fun and use this self-discovery guidance system, the more consistently you'll realize your True Stride.

- You'll know you are aligned with your True Stride when you trust your inner compass to overcome resistance, set your pace and direct your life.

- You'll realize that you've developed muscle memory for the Feel-Choose-Act Amplifier and Wise Walks when you don't require conscious thought to honor your Heart Value, feel appreciated in ways that matter or rhythmically move forward.

- When you take your ability to check in with your feelings, choices and actions for granted, you'll that know your heart is leading you. From that point forward, whatever you do, you will know in your heart-center when you are aligned with your True Stride and when you are not.

FLOURISHING WITH MY SOMETHING

Believe it or not, I didn't set out to write *this* book. Initially, I felt called to write a book about how to authentically voice your value and be memorable, like Paul Revere.

That book also had practical steps toward understanding your value so as to increase your confidence and visibility. The teaching points and stories were relatable and thought-provoking, but my *something* was missing. My *head* had expertise on how to address that much needed topic, but my *heart* longed for *something* more.

AJ Harper is a developmental editor and publishing strategist, and founder of Top

Three Book Workshop. She empowers authors to "Write a book that changes lives, including your own." That's AJ's motto. I am one of her students, and so thankful that we both knew intuitively that my life was not going to change if I published that original book idea.

She kept challenging me to put *you*, my reader, first. AJ would ask, "Who is this book for? What do they need to know? And does the thought of spending the next several years of *your life* with this reader excite you?"

Whoa! What an eye-opening question. Do I want talented, well-deserving individuals of all ages to get the credit they deserve? Yes, absolutely! But praise, kudos and awards alone are not what makes my heart happy.

I love empowering individuals to feel energized by their value and emotionally connected to who benefits from the gifts they choose to share. As we've discussed, feeling appreciated in ways that matter is far more rewarding than any crystal award or accolade. My *something* included surrounding myself with individuals whose hearts crave more meaningful relationships, joy and fulfillment. That's who I want to spend the rest of my life with.

I recall talking to AJ about my belief that honoring your value leads to increased confidence and visibility, and has the power to increase personal fulfillment, appreciation and joy. In other words, *this* book was the one tugging at my heartstrings. I vividly remember her reaction the first time I articulated my *something* after working for months on rewriting my core message. We were on a Zoom call, and she laughed out loud, slapped her desk and said, "Heck yes, who doesn't want that?!"

This book is designed to help you recognize the difference between your heart-centered and your brain-responsive decisions. The more we are in communication with our hearts, the more our feelings can guide us.

I knew that this book was going to be more complex and scarier for me to write

MARY TESS ROONEY

because in my past professions, I had primarily led with logic, data, strategy and tactics. Even though I knew in my heart of hearts that this book was possible and true, my new calling as an author meant switching gears midlife to stretch outside my comfort zone and develop my heart-centered muscle.

The good news for both of us is, I kept channeling Mom's "Show up and let God do the rest" wisdom. I knew that in time, my natural period of resistance would eventually lead to self-discovery and the meaningful, life-changing connection I wanted to make with you.

Writing *Heart Value* has changed my life and revealed my *something*, which is a life of unlocking Heart Value so I can feel appreciated in ways that matter and discover my True Stride. The entire experience has been powerful in so many unexpected ways.

I know there are a lot of different ideas in this book to support you, internally and externally. Honestly, I melded both book ideas into one, because you deserve *this* and *that*. It's not lost on me that at different points in your life, you may gravitate toward one concept more than another depending on your inner compass. What's great is that you can refer back to this book at any time and decide what resonates for you.

Keeping with our adventure theme, you have a unique opportunity to learn from the other adventurers in this book. It's been personally fulfilling to witness individuals who once felt disconnected, deflated and unappreciated for their value as they transform their lives in order to live their most EPIC adventure.

The biggest shift in my own adventure occurred when I stopped allowing others to influence my perspective, redirect my path and shift my priorities based on their agenda. As a Heart Value expert, I am so excited about how I show up every day and my plans for the future. In case you are curious, my design for my EPIC (Envision, Plan, Implement, Cherish) adventure includes:

I *envision* writing a book for kids and teens based on this *Heart Value* book. The lessons and principles apply to people of all ages, and I'm called to nurture the development of young Heart Value muscles.

I *envision* speaking to a room of energetic and optimistic individuals about Heart Value and watching them smile and expand as they realize their True Stride. I see our meeting breaks and evening activities fueled with healthy options for participants to ground in nature and nourish their bodies.

I *envision* retreat centers throughout the world sending out marketing materials on the Heart Value and True Stride programs hosted at their amazing venues.

I *envision* progressive companies booking me as a keynote speaker for their offsite meetings at a playful ski resort, by a national park or on a mountain or beachside with fun outdoor excursion options nearby.

I *envision* schools and universities requesting that I come and inspire our younger generations to become their own Heart Value experts.

I *plan* to network and connect with key contacts and influencers to support my vision.

I *plan* to prioritize fun, and enjoy cross-country road trips in my van to explore national parks with my German shepherds, Cali and Trooper, and I am excited to bond and laugh with some Heart Value relationships along the way.

I *implement* my Joy Frequency Grid activities daily and prioritize fun even at those times when adulting and Distraction Bombs want to occupy my day.

I *implement* my vision and plans with the help of individuals who live by their Heart Value rules. They understand what lights them up. Their talents and contributions energize me and everyone we serve. I know my *something* is more than I want to handle alone, so I'm grateful for our Heart Value connection and their incredible expertise and fun-loving partnership as we envision, plan, implement and cherish our strides together.

I *cherish* every expansion experience and emotional contrast in honor of Mom's words: "Learn all you can; it's money in the bank."

MARY TESS ROONEY

I *cherish* every Wise Walk, win, expansion experience and milestone with you. I feel honored that you chose to read this book, and hope you act on the checkpoints, challenges and practices that resonate with you.

Because of you, I have even more grit to go for the gold and continually invest in my Value Vault.

I know this is only the beginning, but it already feels like I've arrived and the possibilities for the future are endless.

Please don't think this journey is all roses and devoid of any bumps in the road. Like Olympic athletes, even Heart Value experts have tough days, frustrating injuries and unfortunate setbacks. The key is to prioritize your Heart Value, every single day.

Remember, your Heart Value relationships are excited to cheer you on! In fact, they admire you and the example you set. They want you to win the gold for your life's work. Let's face it, we all win when you share your amazing Heart Value with this world.

As you start to plan your EPIC adventure, don't lose sight of your *something*. If you struggle to find your stride, that's okay. If you have to reroute, that's okay. It takes time to embrace your power, but you got this.

When I hit my True Stride—in running and in life—I always feel invincible. I am completely attuned to my entire being, in a groove and deeply rooted in what matters. When I follow my heart, stay true to myself and connect with those who energize and appreciate me, quirks and all, I naturally align with my True Stride.

In my stride, I reap the benefits of feeling strong, empowered and peaceful as I rhythmically move forward. And what's cool is, the vibration and momentum generated in one area of my life carries into other areas too.

You too deserve to be aligned with your True Stride. The most effective way I know to realize your True Stride is to unlock your Heart Value, which fuels more appreciation, meaningful relationships and joy.

As you reflect, notice your emotional responses. Each heart-centered feeling that surfaces provides clues that will influence your choices and inform your actions.

Instrumental Insights

- It's your responsibility to apply your takeaways from this book to reclaim your power, reaffirm your value and activate appreciation in ways that matter most to *you*.

- You are the expert on you, and you get to create your short- and long-term checkpoints along the way.

- The key elements of a Wise Walk are: Alone time in a nurturing space; courage to seek answers to your heartfelt questions; nonjudgment and acceptance to explore what's possible about your *something*.

- Take time to enjoy your version of a Wise Walk to slow down, check your current reality and trust your inner compass to feel, choose and act with intention.

- The biggest shift in your own adventure occurs when you stop allowing others to influence your perspective, redirect your path and shift your priorities based on their agenda.

- In your True Stride, you feel strong, happy and peaceful as you share your Heart Value and feel appreciated in ways that matter.

WISE WALK REFLECTION

Journal without judgment and process these Wise Walk questions to gain awareness.

1. Do you recognize how you feel when you lead with your heart versus your brain-responsive decisions? The more we are in communication with our hearts, the more our feelings can guide us.

2. What is one choice you can make that will honor your *something* more than your natural brain-responsive focus can? How will you choose to create a consistent practice to honor your Heart Value and reclaim your power?

3. Did you do something today that made you feel energized and aligned with your True Stride?

FEEL-CHOOSE-ACT AMPLIFIER

Observe an area in your life that you'd like to address and apply this feel, choose and act approach. Jump right in, or read the following examples to get your Feel-Choose-Act juices flowing.

Feel	Choose	Act

Feel	Choose	Act
Writing that book felt safe and comfortable, but writing this book lights me up.	I evaluated both choices and made my heart-centered choice.	I bravely took action to write this book. It wasn't always easy. I've had to take a million small steps to pursue my something, but I'm happy I followed my heart.

Affirmation

I live my EPIC adventure according to my Heart Value rules and trust my inner compass, every day, as I bravely step toward my *something*.

Tip:

The best gift you can give yourself is to create a safe space or routine to check in and speak your heart-centered truth. What place or activity allows you to decompress and check in with yourself? I cherish my Wise Walks, a bath or a drive that offers uninterrupted alone time. Take a moment to identify the environment(s) that help you slow down, check your reality and engage your inner compass to feel, choose and act with intention. Then schedule consistent time to honor that sacred space for yourself.

Notes:

Get Your Stride On

Energetically and emotionally, you know,
sense and feel when something is off, but
you have to develop that muscle memory
to read your signs and identify
your something.

MARY TESS ROONEY

CHAPTER 11

LIFE BY *YOUR* HEART VALUE RULES

A feeling of personal satisfaction, excitement and hope vibrates through your entire being as you read the signs, direct your path and get your stride on!

Staring at the breathtaking view from the mountain you just climbed, a wave of joy rushes over you. This past year—since you made your Heart Value a priority—has flown by.

You smile in awe. Not just at the beauty of nature that surrounds you, but the life you've intentionally created for yourself and your Heart Value connections.

You reflect on how clunky this perspective felt to start. You were so hard on yourself at first. It was challenging to accept that you had been living according to others' made-up rules of value. It wasn't until you learned to listen to your heart and trust your inner compass that you were able to develop new muscle memories of increased confidence, visibility, joy and earning potential.

For a moment, you wonder what your life would be like if you didn't push past your initial discomfort to honor your *something* that makes your heart happy. Would you still be offering value that pleases others, but makes you cringe inside? Would you still be mindlessly sharing your value with individuals who validate your gifts instead of genuinely appreciating them? Would you still feel too shy or embarrassed to toot your own horn, even if you were tired of getting overlooked?

Then you take a deep breath and again center your thoughts on today. In this moment, none of those questions matter; you did unlock your Heart Value to feel more appreciated in ways that matter. You did take steps, however small, to use your heart-centered feelings to make choices and take actions that aligned with your True Stride.

Your heart is still racing, pounding loudly from the steep climb you made to get here, but it's energized and emotionally fueled by your *something*. Your overall sentiment is, "Wow, I love my life and the transformational Heart Value relationships that surround me."

As you sip water, your smile grows as you appreciate the view and the many paths you took to feel so vibrant and aligned. A year ago, you didn't know this constant feeling of meaningful connection to yourself and others was possible. Now, you can't imagine living any other way.

You have never felt more alive and excited to prioritize fun. You are grateful that your *something*, which you now recognize as your Heart Value, has become a treasured part of your EPIC adventure.

Sure, it's been a wild adventure, filled with a lot of twists and turns, but you cherish every expansion experience as an accrual of value. You feel empowered every time you invest in your Value Vault. And you love your freedom to choose again as you trust your inner compass to become more of who you are and long to be.

MARY TESS ROONEY

Today's Wise Walk reflection reminds you to fearlessly continue to *live by your Heart Value rules*. You anticipate that life will throw you curveballs, but you have learned to revere them as part of your growth and expansion.

Plus, you know that you and your Heart Value relationships will handle them successfully. Your life's work and ability to prioritize fun keep you grounded in who and what, in your life, lights you up.

As you look ahead, you *envision* the next vista that you *plan* to *implement* and *cherish*. A feeling of personal satisfaction, excitement and hope vibrates through your entire being as you begin your descent and pick a path that feels right. All the while, you think about how much easier it is now to read the signs, direct your path and get your stride on!

CHECKPOINT: LIFE BY *YOUR* HEART VALUE RULES

As you reflect, notice your emotional responses. Each heart-centered feeling that surfaces provides clues that will influence your choices and inform your actions.

Instrumental Insights

- Change is not easy. You may need to push past initial discomfort to honor your *something*.

- Meaningful emotional and energetic connection to yourself and others is possible.

- You fearlessly live by your Heart Value rules to honor your EPIC adventure.

- You constantly gain value as you age and give yourself the freedom to choose again.

WISE WALK REFLECTION

Journal without judgment and process these Wise Walk questions to gain awareness.

1. As you envision yourself on the metaphorical mountaintop, what emotions surface for you? How does it make you *feel*?

2. To live by your Heart Value rules, what's one *choice* you are excited or compelled to make today?

3. What *action* empowers you to unlock your Heart Value and get closer to your *something*?

FEEL-CHOOSE-ACT AMPLIFIER

Observe an area in your life that you'd like to address and apply this feel, choose and act amplifier. Jump right in, or read the following examples to get your Feel-Choose-Act juices flowing.

Feel	Choose	Act

| Feel | Choose | Act |

Feel	Choose	Act
You feel aware and accepting of the fact that life will throw you curveballs and unexpected detours.	You choose to cherish and embrace all expansion experiences as an accrual of value.	You invest in your Value Vault daily and proactively activate appreciation for your Heart Value.

Affirmation

I love my life and the transformational Heart Value relationships that surround me.

Tip:

The Bonus Adventures that follow this chapter are opportunities to apply what you've learned throughout this book. Review them to familiarize yourself with what's available to you. I recognize that each of us are unique, so select the adventures that appeal to you. Each choice and action you take will strengthen your Heart Value muscles. And remember, you don't have to do them all or all at once. You get to set your pace and priorities each step of the way. And you can revisit this book and the bonus adventures to your heart's content.

Notes:

Get Your Stride On

Your life's work and ability to prioritize fun keep you grounded in who and what, in your life, lights you up.

BONUS
ADVENTURES

ADVENTURE 1: HEART VALUE DISCOVERY GUIDE

235

- ~ Your adventure kick-off to get you excited about the bonuses available to you in the pages that follow.

- ~ Reminders, reflections and resources to help you apply *Heart Value*'s key themes and the Feel-Choose-Act Amplifier.

ADVENTURE 2: HEART VALUE ZONE

241

- ~ Self-reflection questions to identify how you currently feel about your value, relationships and joy.

- ~ List your top priorities to address opportunities to increase your Heart Value Zone.

ADVENTURE 3: INVEST IN YOUR VALUE VAULT

253

- ~ Document your Value Vault: collect, organize and display your professional accomplishments, personal achievements and expansion experiences in a tangible form (on paper or electronically).

~ Surface emotional contrast to chart how you feel, and illustrate what value is aligned with your future plans. Your efforts will act as a strategic guide to emphasize the Heart Value that fulfills you.

ADVENTURE 4: CREATE YOUR JOY FREQUENCY GRID

~ Your opportunity to use my Joy Frequency Grid as a template to articulate the habits that energize your soul, awaken your heart and fuel your body.

~ Craft your own grid: Trust your inner compass and use your creativity to document the themes and categories that light you up so you can mindfully honor them on a daily basis.

ADVENTURE 5: CHALLENGES

~ Challenges offer us an opportunity to awaken and see what we're capable of.

~ The challenge ideas include: prioritize fun date, trust your inner compass, Heart Value connection, Heart Vibe hunt, invest in your Value Vault and Activate Appreciation.

~ Each is designed to help you apply what you've learned throughout the book; visit www.marytessrooney.com to stay connected to the Striders' collective as that content becomes available and relevant to your life.

~ Designate a predetermined length of time of your choosing for your challenges, based on your unique desires and needs. Then regularly follow through on your intention to achieve your desired

MARY TESS ROONEY

goals. For example, once a day for seven days, I will notice what awakens my Heart Vibe. I will journal about my Heart Vibe Hunt daily to give gratitude and increase my joy frequency.

ADVENTURE 6: PICK-A-PATH THOUGHT STARTERS

- Explore ideas and opportunities to increase your confidence, visibility, joy or earning potential and design your own EPIC adventure.

HEART VALUE DISCOVERY GUIDE

Yippee! I'm so excited that you decided to explore the bonus adventures. I love that you are making *you* a priority!

If you haven't yet figured it out, I like options and the ability to choose my own adventure. I have learned so much about myself through trial, experience and error. With each choice and action, I trust my inner compass to follow my heart as much as my head.

One of my superpowers is my ability to take a deep breath, put myself out there and begin, exactly as I am. I don't shy away from my beginner status. I've learned to take any new adventure, path or trail in stride, because finding my groove is impossible if I don't begin.

Each of us is unique, so only you know your starting point, bandwidth, heart's desires and priorities. Where you start is not important. Your commitment to start and invest time in yourself is what matters.

Even professional athletes were once beginners. We all have to start somewhere before we can gain confidence and momentum to discover our True Stride.

With focus, attention and practice, a beginner has the potential to become advanced. If you start off as advanced, *awesome*…but you'll still need focus, attention and practice to progress to the level of expert. This cycle of beginner, advanced and expert applies to everything we do.

YOUR DISCOVERY GUIDE AT A GLANCE

Since this book is packed with ideas and opportunities for you to unlock your Heart Value, feel appreciated in ways that matter and discover your True Stride, this Heart Value Discovery Guide gives you the takeaways at a glance. Apply the key themes of Read the Signs, Direct Your Path and Get Your Stride On, along with the Feel-Choose-Act Amplifier to enhance your self-discovery practice. I've also included *reflection* and *resource* reminders to support your efforts to develop your muscle memory.

Your *feelings* are clues that influence your *choices* and inform your *actions*. When you understand how your choices and actions make you feel, you can invite more of the good stuff and refine or weed out the stuff that drains or depletes you.

Your Feel-Choose-Act Amplifier is a muscle that strengthens over time. The more you trust your inner compass, the easier it becomes to move in the direction you want to go. As you walk in your truth, you'll receive the synchronicities that align with your *something*. That's your True Stride.

MARY TESS ROONEY

Feel
Choose
Act

Trust Your
Inner Compass

FEEL-CHOOSE-ACT AMPLIFIER: TRUST YOUR INNER COMPASS

Read the Signs > *Feel*: What I've learned, from my own experiences and in working with others, is that what you *feel*—in your *heart*—powerfully reveals your *something*. Since every person, interaction, thing and situation elicits an emotional response, you have the ability to notice what brings you joy, makes your heart happy, dims your light or drains your energy.

- ~ **Reflection:** How do you *feel* about your past, present and future? What energetic and emotional responses surface? As you evaluate your feelings, ask yourself: What's your current reality, and do you feel aligned with where you want to go?

- ~ **Self-discovery resources:** Unlock Your Heart Value, Invest in Your Value Vault, Read the Signs, Wise Walks, Heart Value Zone (Adventure 2)

Direct Your Path > *Choose*: You and your heart are the center of your life force, and external elements—people, places, activities and things—surround you. Direct Your Path theme and your ability to choose, represents you in relation to everything in life that you have to navigate through, around or amongst. It's the paths you believe are available to you based on your own desires, imagination, confidence and courage. Create space to overpower the external influences that may accidently steer you in the wrong direction.

- ~ **Reflection:** What possible paths and resonant choices are available to you? Are you choosing your own adventure or reacting to external pressures and expectations? What is possible for you now, and are you open to other options that present themselves as you move forward?

- ~ **Self-discovery resources:** Design Your EPIC adventure, Pick-a-path Thought Starters (Adventure 6)

Get Your Stride On > *Act*: As you *act* with intention, synchronicities between what you seek and attract will naturally occur. Your action, based on authentic alignment, rewards you with magnetic results. The energy and emotion you put out there comes back to you.

- ~ **Reflection:** What actions expand your True Stride momentum so that you attract more of what and who lights you up energetically and emotionally? Commit to taking one step, however small, to move closer to your dream destination. How does this action move you closer to your *something*?

- ~ **Self-discovery resources:** Activate Appreciation using your contacts, calendar and communications channels; Challenges (Adventure 3)

START WHERE YOU ARE TO ADVANCE TO THE NEXT LEVEL

When I see an opportunity to personally grow or expand, I consider my EPIC adventure method of envision, plan, implement and cherish. Yes, I'm that person who likes to visualize what I want and how I want to feel throughout that experience. Then I figure out what realistic steps are necessary to develop that new muscle, strengthen my mindset or adopt a new behavior.

While I fancy myself a bit of a pioneering woman, I know the power of researching how others have successfully done it before me. It doesn't mean I'll take their path—that's the pioneer in me—but their experience might be a great reference point for learning, listening to my inner compass and following my Heart Value. Or, if their path resonates with me, I'm not too proud to follow their example. As long as it sparks my Heart Vibe, I am open to guidance on how to safely and realistically try new things. The key is to start, just as I am, trust my inner compass and learn as I advance to the next level.

Similar to the way every experience is an accrual of value, each adventure you take builds your muscle memory. I'm naturally curious, so as I search for adventures that matter to me, I'm confident I'll strengthen my True Stride with each step I take.

Depending on where you are, what you want and how you want to feel, you decide which adventure, challenge or pick-a-path resonates with you. Explore, exercise and develop the muscles that you are interested in flexing.

Remember, you are the expert on you. Pay attention to what feels right to you. Have fun with these tools and resources as a way to boost and expand your Heart Value and True Stride.

This is your life. Play by your Heart Value rules as you:

~ Commit to adventures, challenges and paths that resonate with you

- Adopt new perspectives and mindsets

- Develop your muscle memory

- Feel, choose and act with intention

- Expand and apply your abilities

As you take time to strengthen these muscles, you literally amplify your Heart Value as well as more fulfillment, joy, meaningful relationships and appreciation in your life. Enjoy the process and be sure to prioritize fun as you read the signs, direct your path and get your stride on!

HEART VALUE ZONE

YOU ARE HERE

The Heart Value Zone is one tool you can use to assess your starting point. Use the following prompts to surface your heart-centered responses and identify what areas you want to prioritize. Pay attention to any emotions or sensations to help orient your inner compass. Uncover your feeling clues about experiences, past and present, to influence your choices and inform your actions.

HEART VALUE ZONE CHECKPOINT

Good news: It doesn't matter where you start, only that you take inventory to determine what's necessary to increase your Heart Value Zone! After you determine your Heart Value

Zone for each section, you can clearly prioritize where to focus your energy to elevate your value, relationships and joy frequency. I'm excited to begin this adventure with you!

Read each statement. For each row, circle the number from the three-point scale of *Not like me at all* to *Definitely like me* that represents how you feel regarding that statement.

Section 1: Understand Your Heart-Centered Value	Not like me at all	Kind of like me	Definite-ly like me
1. I see my value.	1	2	3
2. I appreciate how my contributions positively impact others.	1	2	3
3. I take time to reflect on my efforts and appreciate my personal growth and expansion daily.	1	2	3
4. I document and showcase my value at least once a week.	1	2	3
5. I pay attention to my energetic and emotional responses to the value I offer.	1	2	3

MARY TESS ROONEY

6. When I notice contributions that drain me, I consider making changes to offer value that energizes me.	1	2	3
7. In the last six months, I rarely felt overlooked, passed over or ignored.	1	2	3
8. I easily accept praise.	1	2	3
9. Without prompting, I take credit for my contributions and in doing so set a good example for the younger generation in how to honor their own value.	1	2	3
10. I am proud to promote my contributions, and illustrate my worth using tangible examples and concrete results at least once a week.	1	2	3

Your value, your relationships and your joy frequency are highest and most resonant with a maximum score of *three*. A score of *one* means you overlook your value, feel unappreciated or disconnected in your relationships and prioritize responsibilities or work above fun in your life, reducing your joy frequency.

For the **Understand Your Heart-Centered Value** section, which statements do you need to prioritize and nurture to be able to respond *Definitely like me*? List the areas of focus you intend to address and journal why this is important to you.

Heart-Centered Value areas to address	Why is this important to you?

MARY TESS ROONEY

Section 2: Appreciate How Your Value Connects with Others and Impacts Your Relationships	Not like me at all	Kind of like me	Definite-ly like me
1. I feel appreciated for my value at work or school.	1	2	3
2. I feel appreciated for my value at home and in my community (neighborhood, social relationships, networks, interest groups, extracurricular activities, hobbies, church, followers, etc.).	1	2	3
3. People closest to me see and appreciate my value, and I don't sacrifice my own happiness for what pleases them.	1	2	3
4. I feel an emotional and energetic connection to the people who benefit from my value (managers, family, friends, coworkers, neighbors, etc.).	1	2	3

5. I ensure that the value I offer others provides me with personal satisfaction and joy.	1	2	3
6. I prioritize my own fulfillment over external expectations and pleasing others.	1	2	3
7. The value I exchange with others feels reciprocal and synergetic. Mutual respect is reflected back to me every day.	1	2	3
8. Because I choose to surround myself with people who genuinely appreciate my value, I set a good example for younger generations.	1	2	3
9. I promote the value I offer and receive some form of appreciation every day.	1	2	3
10. I have a proactive plan to take thoughtful action, at least once a week, to publicize my worth (via social media, email, newsletters, etc.).	1	2	3

For **Your Heart Value Relationships** section, which statements do you need to prioritize and nurture to be able to respond *Definitely like me*? List the areas of focus you intend to address and journal why this is important to you.

Your Heart Value Relationships areas to address	**Why is this important to you?**

Section 3: Acknowledge How Your Efforts to Prioritize Fun Affect Your Joy Frequency	Not like me at all	Kind of like me	Definite- ly like me
1. I am excited to start my day every morning.	1	2	3
2. I deliver value that is personally fulfilling every day.	1	2	3
3. I make choices to prioritize fun every day.	1	2	3
4. I follow my heart-center to live in alignment with choices and actions that bring me joy.	1	2	3
5. I am aware of the activities in my life that energize or drain me.	1	2	3
6. I intentionally and daily make choices and take actions that empower me on an energetic and emotional level to fuel my joy frequency.	1	2	3

7. I don't think that fun and joy are reserved for vacation, or treats, once all my "work" or personal "to-do" lists are accomplished.	1	2	3
8. I don't allow my sense of responsibility to outweigh my need to have fun and experience joy. I have a healthy balance, which helps me serve as a great role model for younger generations.	1	2	3
9. I believe personal satisfaction and external appreciation can coexist. I can be successful and experience joy simultaneously.	1	2	3
10. I review and recall my daily joys prior to falling asleep each night.	1	2	3

For **Your Joy Frequency** section, which statements do you need to prioritize and nurture to be able to respond *Definitely like me*? List the areas of focus you intend to address and journal why this is important to you.

Your Joy Frequency areas to address	Why is this important to you?

MARY TESS ROONEY

Your responses for each section provide insights into how you see and understand your value in relationship to yourself and others, as well as your level of joy frequency. Your top two priorities provide opportunities for you to nurture your Heart Value and increase your joy.

Now that you understand where you want to prioritize fun and elevate your relationships and joy, apply what you've learned throughout this book to do what makes your heart happy. In the next chapter, you will find additional challenges and opportunities to help improve your Heart Value Zone and invest in your Value Vault.

INVEST IN YOUR VALUE VAULT

For the Value Vault challenge, give yourself a quiet, nurturing space to reflect, be creative and capture your gems without judgment, negative thoughts or limited beliefs. There is no right or wrong way to complete this exercise. The learning objectives and questions are your opportunity to trust your inner compass, connect with your adventurous spirit and enjoy creatively producing what feels natural to you.

There is innate power in documenting your value and emotional triggers to chart your future plans. Your efforts will expand your mind and act as a strategic guide as you successfully manage life's unexpected events, impasses and crossroads.

Document your Value Vault: Collect, organize and display your professional accomplishments, personal achievements and expansion experiences on paper. If it seems overwhelming, start with one item for each category.

Remember, all experiences—good, bad, ugly and complicated—expand your value! Don't be shy about listing any that have impacted you and increased your worth, whether you feel positive, negative or neutral about them. Tangible examples to showcase your gems include, but are not limited to:

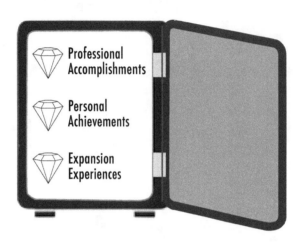

- **Professional accomplishments:** Milestones (successes and failures), certifications, trainings, awards, promotions, applied knowledge, projects, hands-on experiences, impactful lessons, mentor and mentee relationships, crisis management

- **Personal achievements:** Community or church involvement, hobbies, extracurricular activities (races, sports, teams), passions, entertainment interests, life events (geographic moves, kids, marriage), health goals (fitness, medical milestones)

- **Expansion experiences:** Any life event that impacts you. YES, devastating detours and hurtful hiccups too: loss, health challenges, divorce, miscarriage, environmental elements (hurricanes, weather damage), tragedy

Tangible Example	Value Gained	Emotional Contrast	Heart Value (Y/N)
Professional:			
Personal:			
Expansion:			

REMINDERS

~ Use tangible examples: Reflect, document and describe the following in enough detail to fully appreciate each experience.

~ From your earliest memories to now, what personal, professional and expansion experiences have shaped you as a person and the value you offer this world? Keep in mind that our unique upbringing, struggles, wins, failures, triumphs, challenges and successes all increase our Heart Value.

~ The value you have accumulated is your story to tell, in whatever creative format you choose to share.

~ There is innate power in documenting your value and emotional triggers to chart your future plans.

~ Note: Your Value Vault can be a visual timeline (linear or nonlinear), a mind map of scattered moments, a dossier organized by bullet points or themes or a timeline or a chart similar to what was illustrated in Chapter 4.

- IMPORTANT: This is for your reference only, so do what feels natural to YOU.

WISE WALK QUESTIONS FOR THE VALUE VAULT CHALLENGE

Once your Value Vault has tangible examples and emotional contrast, here are a few questions to help you process the amazing visual representation of what made you, *you*. Consider each question and then commit to answering three of them. Self-reflection is a muscle that needs to be consistently worked in order to get stronger.

- As you review your Value Vault, are there any themes that stand out?

- What patterns surfaced that have benefited your growth?

- What patterns surfaced that weigh you down or make you cringe?

- What experiences bring you joy?

- What experiences will you accept, forgive and release to redesign your present and future?

- As you stand in the present, what feelings do you want to repeat and create? What lights you up?

- What behavior (muscle memory) do you need to continue to exercise to align with your heart-center?

- If money or circumstances were not factors, what aspiration (based on your Value Vault exercise) most appeals to you?

- What is your biggest roadblock?

- What strategies will help you anticipate and overcome obstacles?

- What actions will you take to move closer to your desired state and True Stride?

Take this step to invest in your Value Vault and you'll be well on your way! It's time for you to get your Stride on!

DESIGN YOUR JOY FREQUENCY GRID

In Chapter 6, you read my nine daily themes that fuel my body, awaken my heart and energize my soul. As a reminder, my joy frequency is highest when my daily actions incorporate these elements: root, purpose, contribute, meditate, reflect, manifest, exercise, nourish and express. Do you have daily practices that elevate your joy frequency?

Create your own Joy Frequency Grid document, drawing or picture to visually remind you of what you want to experience each day. You are the expert on you, so you may have one priority a day—or twelve. Your joy frequency triggers are unique to you, so structure and name them based on your inner compass.

List your daily habits that elevate your Joy Frequency:

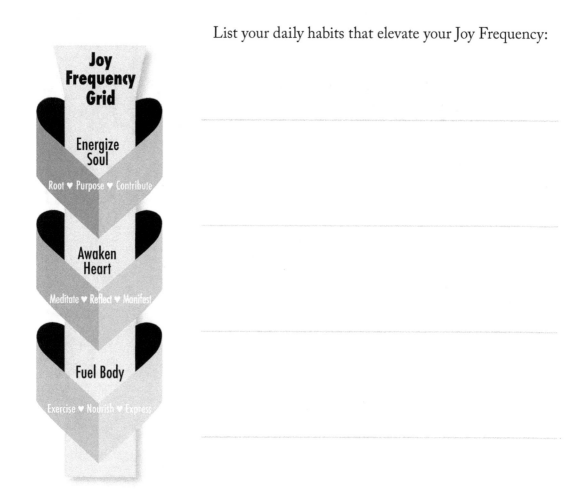

Joy Frequency Grid

Energize Soul

Root ♥ Purpose ♥ Contribute

Awaken Heart

Meditate ♥ Reflect ♥ Manifest

Fuel Body

Exercise ♥ Nourish ♥ Express

Prioritize FUN across all checkpoints!!

WISE WALK QUESTIONS FOR JOY FREQUENCY

Review the following questions and journal your observations related to prioritizing fun, scheduling joytime and elevating your joy frequency. There are no right or wrong answers. Consider each question and then commit to answering three of them.

- ~ Which areas of your life do you want to prioritize daily? Do you have a spiritual practice or exercise regimen that supports your overall well-being?

- ~ What you do or don't do on any given day impacts your energy. What activities support your highest Heart Vibe?

- ~ Which mental models and beliefs keep you from experiencing more fun or joy?

- ~ When you think about bringing more fun or joy into your life, what thoughts pop up? If you have limiting beliefs, are they really true?

- ~ Are you prioritizing fun in all that you do instead of treating it as an afterthought? Or do you reserve fun for vacations and weekends?

- ~ What shifts can you make to incorporate fun as a mission-critical item?

- ~ At the end of your day, how do you hope to have used your time? Is your day jam-packed and overscheduled, or structured to allow for fun to be part of each activity?

CHALLENGES

Social media, online groups, books, courses and individuals have made challenges of all types, lengths and criteria very popular. I've participated in or created my own challenges to enhance my health, happiness, creativity, spirituality, finances and home.

Personally, I'm a fan of shorter challenges, like the seven-day to thirty-day range. When I'm laser focused on a specific goal in a tight time frame, I find it easier to produce quick wins. If a challenge is too long, I may lose interest—unless it's a weekly challenge that builds to a main event, like my NYC marathon. And yes, I believe my marathon training counts as a challenge, because for over twenty weeks I had to honor my daily commitments as part of my overall plan to safely reach the starting line and successfully cross the finish line.

I define a challenge as anything that awakens you to realize your own capabilities. For example, I didn't know I was capable of running a marathon until I did it. The key is to fully commit to a daily or weekly program to fuel your success. Open your mind, decide to have fun and embrace the challenge to see what's possible for yourself.

Challenges can be whatever your heart desires. And they work best if your heart is in them. How can you expansively step into your power, broaden your abilities and encourage others to do the same?

It doesn't matter whether you are a challenge veteran or newbie. What matters is embracing the challenge mindset to push yourself to learn, expand and grow. You might be surprised by what's possible when you accept opportunities to exercise your physical, mental, emotional and spiritual muscles.

Based on your *something* and what's calling you, you have the ability to incorporate a new lifestyle choice or eliminate an unhealthy habit that no longer serves you. And don't forget, you always have the freedom to choose again, so I'd rather you try and change your mind versus not try at all.

This is your EPIC adventure of your own design and execution. If there's something you want to incorporate into your life or stop doing as a result of reading *Heart Value*, then trust your inner compass and make a plan to take action.

Since I want you to have every opportunity to apply what you've read and realized, I've included simple challenge ideas that you can tackle alone or coordinate with others. Use each challenge as a way to energetically and emotionally value who you are, all you have to offer and what makes your heart happy. Each challenge offers guidance to spark your Heart Vibe, unlock your Heart Value, invest in your Value Vault, Activate Appreciation and discover your True Stride.

If you feel intimidated or nervous, I get it. I have been in your shoes. But if you want to live your most EPIC adventure and feel appreciated in ways that matter, you have to take steps—no matter how small—in that direction.

Remember, there is no wrong way to do this. Envision what realizing the goal of your challenge feels like, and see exactly how you want to experience your definition of success as if it's as good as done. This is your adventure, and your chance to exercise your

MARY TESS ROONEY

Heart Value rules in order to live your best life. Your fellow Striders and I are excited to cheer you on, so visit www.marytessrooney.com to see what evolves as the True Stride movement gains momentum.

PRIORITIZE FUN DATES

- Regularly, and for a predetermined length of time, prioritize and schedule FUN dates with yourself. Make yourself and your happiness a priority and do not let any life circumstance distract you.

- I know life can throw some curveballs, so it's okay if you have to be flexible when the unavoidable happens; but at the end of your challenge you will feel strong and capable of creating, scheduling and honoring fun dates in your life that bring you joy.

- If you seek accountability and community, feel free to post your fun dates on social media. Or engage some friends to join you and start a text chain of your fun experiences so you can support good habits and cheer each other on.

TRUST YOUR INNER COMPASS

- Your heart-centered inner compass is unique to you. Regularly, and for a predetermined length of time, pay attention to experiences in your life and record your feelings, choices and actions as a way to connect with your heart. Consider journaling, drawing or getting creative with photographs as a way to capture these feelings, choices and actions and create awareness.

- This self-reflective look into your past or present feelings, choices and actions will build your muscle memory toward trusting your inner compass and using your heart-centered vibration to intentionally move forward.

- Before you go on any adventure, you must get your bearings, read the signs, check your gear and mark your starting point.

- Once your inner compass is calibrated, you are empowered to trust your direction with more confidence and swagger.

HEART VALUE CONNECTION

- Regularly, and for a predetermined length of time, acknowledge Heart Value relationships in your life. Such energetic and emotional connections demonstrate what's possible and what you deserve, so thank them for sharing a mutual heartfelt connection with you and the value you offer.

- If you are committing to this challenge to be introspective, feel free to privately journal your acknowledgment of your Heart Value relationships. Or you can acknowledge your personal or professional appreciation by way of a phone call, email, handwritten note, social media post or anything else that aligns with your heart.

- If you seek accountability and community, consider posting your Heart Value gratitude on social media.

MARY TESS ROONEY

HEART VIBE HUNT

- Regularly, and for a predetermined length of time, self-reflect and identify experiences that spark your Heart Vibe.

- It can be a personal or professional experience that elevates your Heart Vibe. It can be a moment or activity—unexpected or intentional—that warms your heart. It doesn't matter how the experiences surface, but the act of reflecting and documenting your increased Heart Vibe will raise your joy frequency and remind you of the experiences that awaken your heart.

- Taking time to treasure this high Heart Vibe consistently for your predetermined period of time will help you appreciate and attract more of that feeling.

- If you seek accountability and community, feel free to post your daily Heart Vibe Hunt on social media. Engage some friends to join you and start a text chain of experiences that light you up so you can support awareness and cheer each other on.

INVEST IN YOUR VALUE VAULT

- Regularly, and for a predetermined length of time, document the value you offer and how it makes you feel (energizes/depletes or proud/cringe). Create a visual and tangible record for yourself.

- This value can be personal or professional, something you presently offer, offered in the past or feel called to offer in the future.

- If you seek accountability and community, feel free to post your daily Value Vault investment on social media to proudly showcase the value you offer that lights you up.

- *Note*: I don't recommend publicly sharing the value you offer that drains or depletes you. While this awareness is powerful for you, revealing value that you don't want to offer anymore sends a mixed message. Only publicly promote the Value Vault investments that make your heart happy so you can attract more.

- If publicly sharing your Value Vault investments doesn't resonate with you, feel free to journal about your experience or engage some friends to celebrate the value that lights you up. This will establish an awareness for yourself and others.

ACTIVATE APPRECIATION

- Regularly, and for a predetermined length of time, identify strategies, tactics or actions to voice your Heart Value to audiences that may appreciate what you offer.

- Use your contacts, calendar and communications channels to uncover opportunities to connect with like-minded Heart Value relationships or actively promote your Heart Value with those who might share an emotional and energetic connection with you.

- If your existing network won't energetically support the life you desire, consider joining a club or a group to surround yourself with like-minded individuals with the desired frequency you seek. Don't be shy or afraid about making new friends who energetically and emotionally align with your heart's desires. The more you expose yourself to high-frequency people, the more your frequency will match their vibration.

~ The Heart Value you share can be personal or professional, something you presently offer, offered in the past or feel called to offer in the future.

~ If you seek accountability and community, consider posting your daily Activate Appreciation efforts on social media to voice your value and attract individuals who will genuinely benefit from who you are and all that you offer.

~ Or, if you are still hesitant to toot your own horn, find a public relations advocate in your life who won't be shy about praising your talents. This can be a friend, a family member or anyone who shares a Heart Value connection with you. We all need champions, so if you want to start small, Activate Appreciation in your life with one person who will help you voice your value and receive the credit you deserve.

PICK-A-PATH THOUGHT STARTERS

In Chapter 8, you learned how to design your EPIC adventure (envision, plan, implement and cherish). Now you get to decide which activities and behaviors align with how you want to feel as you move forward. This is your chance to explore how pick-a-path ideas resonate with your desired feeling endgame. Remember to listen to your heart, evaluate your choices and act on the paths that light you up.

Obviously, the possible paths and options are endless. Now it's your turn to decide what feels right to support your dreams with choices, actions and accountability.

As you consider your options, allow the "why" to be feeling and heart-centered. For example, "I commit to running three times a week to *feel* stronger, energized and confident." When I don't want to put on my running shoes, I recall the feeling benefits of strength and confidence to motivate me to follow through. I joined a running club to keep me accountable to myself and others with a similar goal.

If you feel stuck, remember: You are not alone. Identify Heart Value connections in your life who are more experienced and willing to collaborate, provide feedback or help you brainstorm. Reach out to someone with similar experience or goals to create a buddy system. The buddy system is a great way to garner support and overcome obstacles.

Establish realistic milestones and celebrate your ongoing commitment to you. Share your progress, setbacks and sidesteps with others who are also committed to your success. To keep your focus and motivation high, create a reward and recognition system for yourself.

You are living by your own Heart Value rules, which is huge, so take time to acknowledge your dedication, progress and impact. You are accruing value with each step, moment and move! Embrace them as you continue to evolve, grow and advance.

Finally, it's safe to say that not everything will go according to plan, and that's okay. Anticipate your whoopsies, detours and roadblocks as part of your EPIC adventure. Keep moving and adjusting. You'll find a way forward, even if you have to take a sidestep.

PICK-A-PATHS DESIGNED AS THOUGHT STARTERS

Whether you are designing an EPIC adventure or writing an email, I know how hard it is to start from a blank page. The good news is, you don't have to.

Identify one goal that will lead you to your desired *feeling* state. Once you are clear on your desired end state, choose two to three paths that you will prioritize over the next thirty to ninety days to best serve you.

MARY TESS ROONEY

Detail specific choices and actions that you will execute to achieve your goals. Finally, be sure to add accountability.

EXAMPLES TO GET YOU GOING

Feeling goal (desired end state)	Pick Your Paths	Choices and Actions	Accountability
Feel more energetically and emotionally connected to my Heart Value	*Increase earning potential*: Have a side hustle	Offer two private beginner guitar lessons to start; build to four clients after ninety days	Regular check-ins with my mentor Autumn are scheduled
Feel seen and connected to like-minded individuals	*Increase visibility*: Use social media as a platform to share resonant messages	Post a personal experience, win or lesson every Tuesday; reshare a post from someone I respect every Thursday	Brainstorm content ideas with Ella, who is very social media savvy, one month in advance of social posts to have a proactive plan
Feel stronger, braver and healthier	*Increase confidence:* Create a healthy activity schedule	Run three times a week; yoga once a week	Join a running club for company and encouragement to log miles

Feeling goal (desired end state)	Pick Your Paths	Choices and Actions	Accountability
Feel more joyful and energized by activities that light me up	*Increase your joy frequency:* Discover a new joy	Since I enjoy nature, animals and exercise: Take horseback riding lessons once a week	Schedule a weekly lesson and honor my joytime commitment to myself

Increase Your . . .

Confidence

Visibility

Joy Frequency

Earning Potential

PICK-A-PATHS TO INCREASE CONFIDENCE, VISIBILITY, JOY AND EARNING POTENTIAL

I partnered with Leigh Farrow, author of *Leadership Nuts*[19], to list some common and relatable pick-a-path examples in the pages that follow. For inspiration, you'll find some *increased confidence, visibility, joy and earning potential paths* to get you started.

Review the paths as thought starters and notice which ideas excite and energize you! If you are feeling more adventurous, think outside the box and create your own

MARY TESS ROONEY

pick-a-paths. Again, this is your adventure, so design your EPIC adventure according to your Heart Value rules using your heart-centered inner compass.

Thoughts are things, so choose to shift your mindset from resistance to possibilities in order to achieve the EPIC adventure you crave and deserve. Be sure to prioritize what matters most to you. Start small and build momentum with each step you take. Enjoy!!

INCREASE CONFIDENCE: BUILD YOUR SELF-BELIEF

- ~ Gain awareness via self-study

  - ∞ Know your strengths and weaknesses
  - ∞ Conduct a personal brand survey
  - ∞ Identify your negative triggers
  - ∞ Commit to daily self-reflection

- ~ Become the expert

  - ∞ Analyze current knowledge base to determine your own expertise
  - ∞ Read source materials
  - ∞ Speak to other experts
  - ∞ Dedicate time
  - ∞ Create a deliberate practice

- ~ Maintain a positive mindset

  - ∞ Create daily affirmation(s)
  - ∞ Question your inner critic—is it too loud?

∞ Turn a failure into a learning opportunity and move forward

~ Engage a mentor

∞ Create a list of potential mentors within your personal or professional life, adding pros and cons for variables
∞ Commit to a productive meeting schedule with a formal agenda and follow-up communications
∞ Prepare for every conversation

~ Update headshots

∞ Consider personal and professional strategies
∞ Consider: indoor or outdoor?
∞ Create a photo that is authentic to your personal style
∞ Use a photo that provides a narrative

~ Improve self-care: physical, social, emotional

∞ Your self-image has a direct bearing on your confidence level; if so desired, create a healthier lifestyle to have a positive impact
∞ Create an activity schedule—yoga, running, weights, etc.
∞ Engage a dietician and choose foods that boost energy, improve immunity, etc.
∞ Utilize meditation

MARY TESS ROONEY

- ∞ Work with a therapist
- ∞ Stay in touch with people, continue to build relationships

- Improve public speaking

  - ∞ Practice, practice, practice—spend as much time practicing as you do creating content
  - ∞ Videotape yourself—this allows you to discern your tone, pace, body language, etc.
  - ∞ Work with a coach
  - ∞ Avoid filler and transitional words
  - ∞ Learn to read your audience

- Do something for the first time

  - ∞ Push your comfort zone by trying something new
  - ∞ Create small successes by creating a list of easy "first time" challenges and accomplish one after another
  - ∞ Talk to people about their interests and learn about potential opportunities
  - ∞ Get rid of habits and activities that are no longer enjoyable or contribute to your well-being

- Define your personal brand statement

  - ∞ Come up with a short, concise statement that represents who you are and what you believe is true about yourself and your abilities. This is your

individual unique selling proposition

- ∞ Write several statements, and ask for feedback to discern perception versus reality
- ∞ Be authentic; do not overcommit or overstate

- ~ Become an influencer

  - ∞ Choose your niche
  - ∞ Create your brand identity—how do you stand apart?
  - ∞ Determine the tools you will use
  - ∞ Become an expert storyteller (in short spurts and creative captions)

INCREASE VISIBILITY: RAISE YOUR PROFILE

- ~ Serve on committees or participate in special projects—get out of the shadows

  - ∞ Look outside of your job parameters for opportunities
  - ∞ Ask for the opportunity
  - ∞ Research solutions and provide answers

- ~ Build a network

  - ∞ Seek out a mentor
  - ∞ Join corporate work groups and, if unavailable, create one
  - ∞ Be helpful to others

MARY TESS ROONEY

- ∞ Learn to listen
- ∞ Join personal interest groups
- ∞ Follow specific interest groups online
- ∞ Connect with former, past relationships

- ~ Become an industry panelist or speaker

  - ∞ Seek out opportunities to demonstrate your expertise and knowledge
  - ∞ Improve your speaking skills and style
  - ∞ Deliver unique perspective

- ~ Create a marketing plan

  - ∞ Define your brand
  - ∞ Conduct a SWOT (strengths, weaknesses, opportunities, threats) analysis
  - ∞ Establish your marketing objectives
  - ∞ Determine performance measurements

- ~ Create a public relations plan

  - ∞ Detail your goals and your why
  - ∞ Identify your audience (What are they reading and viewing? Where do they gather?)
  - ∞ Determine the outlets you will need to include to reach your specific audience
  - ∞ Create engaging and unique content
  - ∞ Craft your pitch

- ~ Create a social media plan

- ∞ Create a plan to use social media networks, including your why and how
- ∞ Pick the right channels
- ∞ Ensure your profiles are complete
- ∞ Create interesting content
- ∞ Develop a posting strategy
- ∞ Understand metrics analysis and how to determine success

- ~ Become a newsletter contributor

  - ∞ Learn to write effective and memorable content
  - ∞ Learn the art of conversational writing (as if talking with one person)
  - ∞ Limit insider jargon or lexicons

- ~ Write white papers

  - ∞ Determine the audience
  - ∞ Decide on simple versus complex content
  - ∞ Illustrate the problem and offer up a unique solution
  - ∞ Get to the point
  - ∞ Provide a clever title

- ~ Write a blog

  - ∞ Define the area of interest(s)
  - ∞ Select your platform, domain name and hosting partner

- ∞ Read others—understand what makes them good
- ∞ Create content
- ∞ Spark conversation

- ~ Produce a podcast

  - ∞ Define your voice and why others should listen
  - ∞ Listen to other podcasts
  - ∞ Determine where you want to host your podcast
  - ∞ Research and purchase equipment (low barrier to entry)
  - ∞ Record and listen, secure feedback
  - ∞ Understand licensing agreements
  - ∞ Upload content
  - ∞ Get listed with podcast platforms

INCREASE YOUR JOY FREQUENCY: PRIORITIZE FUN!

- ~ Define what brings you joy

  - ∞ Make a list: painting, sports, learning, self-care, cooking, reading, writing, etc.
  - ∞ Act on your joy and choose to commit a specific amount of time to it daily, weekly or monthly

- ~ Discover new joy

  - ∞ List areas of interest you believe would add joy to your life, but have not yet acted upon, for example: pottery, improv, climbing, drum circle, diving, flying, adopt a pet, volunteer, etc.

- ∞ Develop a plan to engage in this new joy journey
- ∞ Commit, engage, discover

~ Start your day with joy moments

- ∞ Joy journal—put your mind on a positive path before the negativity of the day grabs hold
- ∞ Listen to an entertaining, motivational podcast while preparing for the day
- ∞ Read an article of interest; challenge your mind before the repetition of the day begins
- ∞ Sing; affect your heart and soul with nostalgic, energizing or relaxing music
- ∞ Recognize what you do have, express gratitude

~ Create a joy break

- ∞ Take brain breaks, and use them for joyful activities, for example: grab an ice cream cone, take a walk, take a nap, meditate, call a friend, etc.
- ∞ Switch thirty minutes of screen time to joytime— rather than looking at what others are doing, take the time to do something yourself

~ Share the joy

- ∞ Send a handwritten note to someone who has gifted your life in some way
- ∞ Invite a positive influencer to have coffee

MARY TESS ROONEY

- Voice your Value Vault

    - ∞ Compile a list of professional awards and accolades—submit to awards or have others submit on your behalf
    - ∞ Assemble a collection of your achievements for your boss, ensuring that it illustrates your contributions, impact and results
    - ∞ Craft a positive, affirming communication regarding your influence, involvement and impact; share it

- Create a transition plan/exit strategy

    - ∞ Compile a target list of companies for whom you would like to work and develop a strategy
    - ∞ Understand and organize your finances; plan for a transitional period
    - ∞ Carefully consider the exit date; consider payout dates as well as your support structure
    - ∞ Plan your exit; the way you leave will be remembered and may overshadow all that went before

- Ask for a raise, bonus increase or other financial incentives

    - ∞ Prepare by creating a narrative that illustrates your impact, results and contributions

- ∞ Timing is critical; factor in the company budget cycle
- ∞ Create a compensation analysis that is inclusive of market and geographic considerations and salary ranges
- ∞ Formally organize your thoughts; prepare for varying outcomes
- ∞ Get creative: If they can't offer you monetary gains, request more vacation or to be funded for a desired training or certification

- ~ Have a side hustle

  - ∞ Create a supplemental income source, outside the boundaries of your day job, that is built around a passion in your life
  - ∞ Join crowdsourcing, micro jobs to get paid for online or real-world tasks
  - ∞ Become an online teacher or create an online course
  - ∞ Pursue freelance writing
  - ∞ Schedule time for the side hustle; do not let it impact the day job

- ~ Identify and develop new talents and abilities

  - ∞ Investigate new skills and challenges that are of interest to you; hobbies can become revenue contributors

- ∞ Establish goals and commit to a specific amount of time each day to advance your learning
- ∞ Find an online course that will allow you to expand your knowledge
- ∞ Talk to your leadership, express your interest and work with human resources to create a learning strategy

If the increased visibility, earning potential, joy and confidence pick-a-paths don't speak to you, no worries. Grab a friend or trusted mentor or hire a coach to brainstorm choices and actions that will achieve your desired feeling state. You are worth the time and investment in your happiness and fulfillment.

Also, if you create a pick-a-path that will benefit other Striders, please visit www.marytessrooney.com to share your awesome ideas. When your Heart Value rises, you inspire and lift the vibrations of everyone around you.

Feeling goal (desired end state)	Pick-a-path	Choices and Actions	Accountability
Based on what you want, how do you want to feel?	What paths light you up and support your desired feeling state?	What choices and actions are you committing to, and by when? How will you know you got there?	What people or resources will support you to get going (brainstorm and collaborate) and stay the course (accountability and encouragement)?

Endnotes

19   Leigh Farrow, *Leadership Nuts* (United States: Leigh P. Farrow, 2020).

STRIDER'S GLOSSARY OF TERMS

Achilles' heel refers to a quality or characteristic that exposes weakness and vulnerability even in the strongest of people.

Appreciation confirms that you are sharing your value with the right audience, one that has an energetic and emotional connection to you.

Checkpoints are your chance to take a breather, be present, process and apply the chapter's concepts and lessons to your life. They are your opportunity to cherish your aha moments, appreciate how far you've come, acknowledge your expansion, awaken your heart to new possibilities and envision the life you want so you can plan and implement what's next.

Distraction Bombs are unexpected demands, problems, events or dramatic conversations that take you away from your focus and daily objectives.

DNF in adventure race lingo is short for Did Not Finish and means we did not collect all the required checkpoint markers within the time limit.

Emotional contrast means acknowledging the feelings that surface from the value you offer and who benefits from it. Your emotional contrast empowers you to use your desirable past and present responses to help determine your future.

EPIC, in EPIC adventure, stands for Envision, Plan, Implement and Cherish.

Expansion experiences are your life's challenges that prompt you to evolve. Through each uncomfortable lesson, you gain confidence in who you are and who you were meant to be.

Feel-Choose-Act Amplifier is a self-discovery practice you can use to gauge how your feelings influence your choices and inform your actions. When you understand your heart and head connections, you can intentionally invite more feel-good experiences that align with your something.

Heart Value is your energetic and emotional connection to the value you offer that lights you up.

Heart Vibe is your ability to sense how experiences and external elements (people, places, activities and things) awaken your heart or dim your light.

Instrumental Insights follow each chapter to reinforce the key messages and takeaways.

Joy Frequency refers to the level at which your vibration radiates harmony and blissful energy, inward and outward. Your goal is to have a high amount and occurrence of joy felt in your life, which means you consistently do things that light you up.

Joytime is a scheduled date or commitment to yourself to do something that brings you joy.

Muscle memory is a skill and ability that becomes our own unconscious response. It's a movement or pattern that becomes second nature after consistent practice, like brushing your teeth or driving a car.

Negative Nitwits spread gloom and drain others because they are unhappy with themselves and disconnected from their Heart Value.

Pick-a path is your ability to consider available options and select your resonant choice.

Prioritize fun means to reserve, block and protect time in your day to experience joy and awaken your Heart Vibe.

Resonant choice is a decision that aligns with the perspective that feels right to you.

Superpower is a unique talent or ability that makes a valuable impact.

MARY TESS ROONEY

Transactional relationships provide an exchange or interaction without an energetic or emotional connection to your value.

Transformational relationships offer a mutual exchange of Heart Value that feels energizing, fulfilling and rewarding.

True Stride is feeling aligned with your heart in all that you do as you energetically move forward in your truth.

Validation means that your value is desired and makes an impact. Appreciation confirms that you are sharing your value with the right audience, one that has an emotional and energetic connection to you.

Value Vault is an account of all your experiences—your successes, whoopsies and everything in between—that have increased your value and made you, you (including how each experience makes you feel).

Wise Walks are your opportunity to slow down, check your reality and ask questions to gauge your energetic and emotional responses. Each heart-centered feeling provides clues that influence your choices and inform your actions.

MARY TESS ROONEY founded True Stride to create a movement where individuals unlock their Heart Value to deepen personal fulfillment, increase meaningful relationships and elevate joy.

As a Heart Value expert, author and speaker, Mary Tess created strategies and tools to help people like *you* voice your value and prioritize fun. In *Heart Value*, Mary Tess guides readers to recognize what lights them up to feel energized and appreciated in ways that matter.

Mary Tess's love of adventure prompts a "yes" to practically all new opportunities. She loves the outdoors, animals, cooking and physical activities like hiking, horseback riding and skiing. In her search for joy and meaning, Mary Tess attends holistic retreats and explores the national parks with her two German shepherds.

Prior to True Stride, Mary Tess was a strategy and communications executive who naturally sifted through noise, crafted plans, achieved results and enabled teams to *get their stride on* within a multibillion-dollar business. Her business savvy, intuition and proficiency in sales, training, communications, public relations and project management empowers individuals to achieve success based on their own personal vision and Heart Value rules.

Mary Tess holds a Bachelor of Arts degree from New York University and certifications in coaching, change management, executive leadership, sales training, yoga and more. For fun, you'll find her following her heart to design epic adventures and making memories with loved ones.

CPSIA information can be obtained
at www.ICGtesting.com
Printed in the USA
BVHW010741251021
619811BV00012B/377